Domestic Abuse

Editor: Danielle Lobban

Volume 441

First published by Independence Educational Publishers

The Studio, High Green

Great Shelford

Cambridge CB22 5EG

England

© Independence 2024

Copyright

This book is sold subject to the condition that it shall not,
by way of trade or otherwise, be lent, resold, hired out or otherwise
circulated in any form of binding or cover other than that in which it
is published without the publisher's prior consent.

Photocopy licence

The material in this book is protected by copyright. However, the
purchaser is free to make multiple copies of particular articles for instructional
purposes for immediate use within the purchasing institution.
Making copies of the entire book is not permitted.

ISBN-13: 978 1 86168 901 6

Printed in Great Britain

Zenith Print Group

Acknowledgements

The publisher is grateful for permission to reproduce the material in this book. While every care has been taken to trace and acknowledge copyright, the publisher tenders its apology for any accidental infringement or where copyright has proved untraceable. The publisher would be pleased to come to a suitable arrangement in any such case with the rightful owner.

The material reproduced in **issues** books is provided as an educational resource only. The views, opinions and information contained within reprinted material in **issues** books do not necessarily represent those of Independence Educational Publishers and its employees.

Images

Cover image courtesy of iStock. All other images courtesy of Freepik, Pexels, Pixabay and Unsplash.

Additional acknowledgements

With thanks to the Independence team: Janey Hills, Klaudia Sommer and Jackie Staines.

Danielle Lobban

Cambridge, May 2024

Contents

Chapter 1: What Is Domestic Abuse?

Domestic abuse	1
What is domestic abuse?	2
The myths	4
The facts	5
Domestic abuse in England and Wales	6
Men can be victims of domestic abuse too	8
Demand for men's domestic abuse helpline almost triples over 5 years	10
Helping male victims of domestic abuse can benefit society as a whole	12
You were told: a voice for killed women	14
Domestic abusers who kill their partners to face tougher sentences	18

Chapter 2: Signs of Abuse

I'm not sure if my relationship is healthy	20
Love-bombing and gaslighting: tactics of domestic abuse	22
How to speak to your partner about gaslighting – and when to end the relationship	23
Why victims of domestic abuse don't leave – four experts explain	24
Mother of teenager murdered by ex warns 'end of a relationship is the most dangerous time in a woman's life'	26
I want to leave my relationship safely	28

Chapter 3: Preventing and Surviving Abuse

Domestic abuse victims to be given up to £2,500 to help them flee partners	31
Tina Turner: the singer's resilience and defiance were typical of a survivor of intimate partner abuse	32
'When you admit the truth, you have to take action': the phoneline helping abusers change their behaviour	34
'The law is cold. It doesn't reflect the life lost': mothers of murdered women tell their stories	36
Asha's story	37
What is Clare's Law?	38
Is Clare's Law working?	39
'Sally's Law'	40

Useful Websites/Where can I find help?	42
Glossary	43
Index	44

Introduction

Domestic Abuse is Volume 441 in the **issues** series. The aim of the series is to offer current, diverse information about important issues in our world, from a UK perspective.

About *Domestic Abuse*

Every year, approximately 2 million individuals in the UK suffer from some type of domestic abuse. This book looks at different types of abuse, explores facts, statistics and myths surrounding the issue and considers different approaches to tackling this serious problem.

Our sources

Titles in the **issues** series are designed to function as educational resource books, providing a balanced overview of a specific subject.

The information in our books is comprised of facts, articles and opinions from many different sources, including:

- Newspaper reports and opinion pieces
- Website factsheets
- Magazine and journal articles
- Statistics and surveys
- Government reports
- Literature from special interest groups.

A note on critical evaluation

Because the information reprinted here is from a number of different sources, readers should bear in mind the origin of the text and whether the source is likely to have a particular bias when presenting information (or when conducting their research). It is hoped that, as you read about the many aspects of the issues explored in this book, you will critically evaluate the information presented.

It is important that you decide whether you are being presented with facts or opinions. Does the writer give a biased or unbiased report? If an opinion is being expressed, do you agree with the writer? Is there potential bias to the 'facts' or statistics behind an article?

Activities

Throughout this book, you will find a selection of assignments and activities designed to help you engage with the articles you have been reading and to explore your own opinions. Some tasks will take longer than others and there is a mixture of design, writing and research-based activities that you can complete alone or in a group.

Further research

At the end of each article we have listed its source and a website that you can visit if you would like to conduct your own research. Please remember to critically evaluate any sources that you consult and consider whether the information you are viewing is accurate and unbiased.

Issues Online

The **issues** series of books is complemented by our online resource, issuesonline.co.uk

On the Issues Online website you will find a wealth of information, covering over 70 topics, to support the PSHE and RSE curriculum.

Why Issues Online?

Researching a topic? Issues Online is the best place to start for...

Librarians

Issues Online is an essential tool for librarians: feel confident you are signposting safe, reliable, user-friendly online resources to students and teaching staff alike. We provide multi-user concurrent access, so no waiting around for another student to finish with a resource. Issues Online also provides FREE downloadable posters for your shelf/wall/table displays.

Teachers

Issues Online is an ideal resource for lesson planning, inspiring lively debate in class and setting lessons and homework tasks.

Our accessible, engaging content helps deepen students' knowledge, promotes critical thinking and develops independent learning skills.

Issues Online saves precious preparation time. We wade through the wealth of material on the internet to filter the best quality, most relevant and up-to-date information you need to start exploring a topic.

Our carefully selected, balanced content presents an overview and insight into each topic from a variety of sources and viewpoints.

Students

Issues Online is designed to support your studies in a broad range of topics, particularly social issues relevant to young people today.

There are thousands of articles, statistics and infographs instantly available to help you with research and assignments.

With 24/7 access using the powerful Algolia search system, you can find relevant information quickly, easily and safely anytime from your laptop, tablet or smartphone, in class or at home.

Visit issuesonline.co.uk to find out more!

Chapter 1

What Is Domestic Abuse?

Domestic abuse

Domestic abuse is a serious issue that affects countless individuals, including young people just like you. Have you ever wondered what domestic abuse really is and why it happens? Let's dive into this important topic together!

In this book, we aim to provide you with a clear understanding of domestic abuse. Our goal is to empower you with knowledge so that you can recognise the signs, seek help, and support others who may be going through this difficult experience.

What is domestic abuse?

Domestic abuse is when one person in a family or relationship uses their power to harm another person. It can involve physical harm, like hitting or pushing, but it can also include emotional harm, such as controlling or manipulating someone's feelings. Verbal abuse, like using hurtful words, is another form of domestic abuse.

It's important to remember that domestic abuse is never acceptable, and everyone deserves to feel safe and respected in their relationships.

Types of domestic abuse

Physical abuse: Physical abuse refers to any form of violence that causes harm to another person's body. It can leave bruises, cuts, or even serious injuries. If you or someone you know is experiencing physical abuse, it's important to seek help from a trusted adult or professional immediately.

Emotional abuse: Emotional abuse is when someone uses words or actions to control, humiliate, or manipulate another person's emotions. This can include constant criticism, belittling, or even threats. The impact of emotional abuse can be long-lasting and damaging to a person's mental well-being.

Verbal abuse: Verbal abuse involves the use of hurtful words to demean, intimidate, or degrade another person. It can leave emotional scars that can take a long time to heal. Remember, words have power, and it's important to speak up if you or someone you know is experiencing verbal abuse.

Warning signs of domestic abuse

Recognising the warning signs of domestic abuse is crucial for identifying if someone is in an unhealthy relationship. These signs may include unexplained injuries, changes in behaviour or personality, isolation from friends and family, or constant fear. If you notice any of these signs in yourself or someone else, it's important to seek help and support.

Remember, domestic abuse is not the fault of the person experiencing it. It's important to approach the situation with empathy and offer support without judgement.

Effects of domestic abuse

Domestic abuse can have severe and long-lasting effects on the victims. It can result in physical injuries, such as broken bones or internal damage, but it can also have emotional and psychological consequences. Victims of domestic abuse may experience anxiety, depression, low self-esteem, or even develop post-traumatic stress disorder (PTSD). It's vital to create a safe and supportive environment to help survivors heal and recover.

Where to seek help

If you or someone you know is experiencing domestic abuse, know that you are not alone and help is available. There are some helplines and websites listed on page 42. The professionals behind these are trained to support you and provide guidance through challenging situations.

Additionally, it's crucial to reach out to a trusted adult, such as a teacher, counsellor, or family member if you need immediate help or support. Remember, you don't have to face this alone.

How to support others

If someone you know is experiencing domestic abuse, it's essential to be a supportive friend or family member. Start by actively listening without judgement and letting them know you believe them. Encourage them to seek professional help and provide information about available resources.

It's crucial to prioritise your own safety when offering support. If you feel your safety is at risk, encourage the person experiencing abuse to seek help from professionals who can provide the necessary support and protection.

Conclusion

Domestic abuse is a serious issue that affects individuals of all ages. By understanding what domestic abuse is and how we can help, we can create a safer and more supportive society. Remember, you have the power to make a difference!

Let's raise awareness about domestic abuse, support one another, and work towards building a world where everyone can thrive, free from violence and harm.

What is domestic abuse?

Domestic abuse is abuse that takes place within an intimate or family-type relationship. It can be carried out by a current or ex-partner, their family members, your own family members, or the parent of your child. An abuser might involve other family members, friends or members of the community in their abuse.

Abuse is abuse, whether it consists of a single incident or a long-term pattern of behaviour. The definitions below will help you to understand whether you, or someone you know, is experiencing domestic abuse.

Controlling or coercive behaviour

Coercive control is a pattern of behaviour used by abusers to instil fear and restrict freedom. It underpins all forms of domestic abuse.

Coercive control involves an abuser repeatedly behaving in a way that makes you feel controlled, dependent, isolated, or scared. The following types of behaviour are common examples of coercive control:

- Isolating you from your friends and family;
- Restricting or monitoring your activities and your movements including listening to your phone calls and reading your texts/emails;
- Controlling how much money you have and how you spend it;
- Threatening to report you to social services, the police or immigration services unless you comply with their demands;
- Threatening to take your children away;
- Threatening to share private information with your friends/family/community to shame or embarrass you;
- Preventing you from taking medication or accessing healthcare.

Psychological or emotional abuse

Psychological abuse can be difficult to recognise. It can include:

- Intimidation;
- Name-calling;
- Criticisms and insults made in private or in front of others about your appearance, parenting or cooking/housekeeping;
- Silent treatment;
- Manipulation;
- Blame;
- Gaslighting (creating a false narrative that makes you question your own judgements and reality);
- Making fun of/patronising you when you speak and dismissing you or your concerns as if you are unimportant.

Physical abuse

Physical abuse is the most visible form of domestic abuse. It can lead to permanent injuries, health issues and, at times, death. It can include such behaviour as:

- Pinching, slapping, punching, shaking, burning, kicking, biting, stabbing;
- Pinning you down, holding you by the neck;
- Restraining you;
- Throwing things at you.

Sexual abuse

Sexual abuse involves:

- Using force, threats, or intimidation to make you perform sexual acts;
- Having sex with you when you don't want it;
- Forcing you to look at pornographic material;
- Constant pressure and harassment into having sex when you don't want to;
- Forcing you to have sex with other people;
- Any degrading treatment related to your sexuality.

Economic or financial abuse

95% of cases of domestic abuse involve economic abuse. Economic abuse can take many forms, including:

- Sabotaging your income and access to money by preventing you from going to work or accessing education;
- Taking your wages and making you ask for money;
- Refusing to let you claim benefits;
- Taking children's savings or birthday money;
- Withholding child maintenance payments;
- Dictating what you can buy;
- Checking your receipts;
- Making you keep a spending diary;
- Insisting all savings and assets (e.g. house, car) are in their name;
- Insisting all bills, credit cards and loans are in your name and making you pay the;
- Building up debt in your name with or without your knowledge.

Technological abuse

Abusers often use technology to carry out their abuse. They may use technology to monitor you in your home, track your location, harass you online, record you without your consent or upload sensitive or private information or images or videos of you online.

Harmful practices

Harmful practices are forms of violence which have been committed in certain communities and societies for so long that they are considered, or presented by abusers, to be acceptable cultural practices. Harmful practices include:

- Forced marriage;
- 'Honour' based abuse;
- Female genital mutilation (FGM);
- Gender selective abortion;
- Female infanticide (the deliberate killing of newborn female children);
- Dowry-related violence;
- Acid attacks.

14 March 2023

Write
Write a one-paragraph definition of coercive control.

Write
Write a one-paragraph definition of financial abuse.

The above information is reprinted with kind permission from Southall Black Sisters
© 2024 Southall Black Sisters

www.southallblacksisters.org.uk

The myths

It can be tempting to explain away abusive behaviour by making excuses.

Let's bust some myths, shall we?

It can be tempting to explain away patterns of abusive behaviour but it's important to call that what it is: making excuses.

Remember, there is only one person to blame for abuse – **and that is the abuser**.

Myth 1: Alcohol, drugs, and stress make men violent

Abusers are also violent when sober. Many men who drink never use violence. These are all excuses.

Myth 2: She would leave if it was really bad

There are many overlapping and intersecting reasons why women may stay. Leaving is difficult and takes time. It is a process.

Myth 3: Abusers grow up in violent homes

Violence is a choice an abuser makes; he alone is responsible.

Myth 4: Domestic abuse only happens to certain women

Domestic abuse can happen to any woman regardless of where they live, their profession, or their social, economic or ethnic background.

Myth 5: Some women deserve it

Men often claim their partner 'makes them do it'. This is victim-blaming. The abuser alone is responsible.

Myth 6: He just loses his temper sometimes

Abusers say they 'see red' sometimes – but they are very much in control, using multiple methods to abuse.

Myth 7: Some women like violence

Women do not enjoy violence. Most live in fear and terror. This is victim-blaming.

Myth 8: She's lucky to have him

Whether your abuser is also your caregiver, or presents himself as the perfect breadwinner, women often hear they are lucky to have someone 'looking after them'. But you deserve to make choices about your own life.

Myth 9: Domestic abuse is a private matter

Domestic abuse is a crime. It is not an individual but a social problem. We all need to speak out against it.

Information correct at date of publication, please check the Refuge website at refuge.org.uk for up-to-date information. The above information is reprinted with kind permission from Refuge.

© Refuge 2024

www.refuge.org.uk

The facts

The numbers don't lie: they tell a clear story about the prevalence and harmful effects of abuse.

The facts tell a clear story...

Domestic abuse is all too common in the UK, and its harmful impacts on survivors can extend to many areas of their lives, including mental health, physical well-being and family safety.

Fact: The police receive a domestic abuse-related call every 30 seconds.

Yet it is estimated that less than 24% of domestic abuse crime is reported to the police.

Fact: 1 in 4 women in England and Wales will experience domestic abuse in her lifetime.

Domestic abuse feels incredibly isolating, but the numbers tell a different story: you are not alone.

Fact: On average, 2 women a week are killed by a current or former partner in England and Wales.

If you are afraid of your partner, Refuge is here to help you. Always call 999 in an emergency.

Fact: It takes, on average, 7 attempts before a woman is able to leave for good.

Leaving an abusive partner is a process, not a single act.

Fact: Domestic abuse is linked to depression and homelessness.

Women who experience domestic abuse are twice as likely to experience depression, and 40% of homeless women state domestic abuse as a contributory factor to their homelessness.

Fact: Domestic abuse can lead women to suicide.

It is estimated that around 3 women a week die by suicide as a result of domestic abuse.

Fact: 20% of children in the UK have lived with an adult perpetrating domestic abuse.

That's 1 in 5 kids.

Fact: Domestic abuse gets worse during pregnancy.

About 20% of women in Refuge's services are pregnant or have recently given birth.

Fact: Young girls in the UK report high incidence of sexual violence.

41% of UK girls aged 14 to 17 in an intimate relationship experienced some form of sexual violence from their partner.

Fact: 93% of defendants in domestic abuse cases are male; 84% of victims are female.

And yet, women are three times more likely to be arrested for incidents of abuse.

Fact: Domestic abuse costs the UK an estimated £23 billion a year.

It is not only weighing on our physical and emotional health, but also our economy.

Information correct at date of publication, please check the Refuge website at refuge.org.uk for up-to-date information. The above information is reprinted with kind permission from Refuge.

© Refuge 2024

www.refuge.org.uk

Domestic abuse in England and Wales

An extract.

- The Crime Survey for England and Wales, estimated that 2.1 million people aged 16 years and over (1.4 million women and 751,000 men) experienced domestic abuse in the year ending March 2023.
- There was no significant change in the prevalence of domestic abuse experienced in the last year compared with the previous year.
- The police recorded 889,918 domestic abuse-related crimes (excluding Devon and Cornwall) in the year ending March 2023, a similar number to the previous year.
- There were 51,288 domestic abuse-related prosecutions in England and Wales for the year ending March 2023, compared with 53,207 in the year ending March 2022.

Domestic abuse

Domestic abuse is not limited to physical violence and can include a range of abusive behaviours. It can also be experienced as repeated patterns of abusive behaviour to maintain power and control in a relationship. The Domestic Abuse Act 2021 defines domestic abuse as any incident or pattern of incidents between those aged 16 years and over who:

- Are a partner
- Are an ex-partner
- Are a relative

Figure 1:

Approximately one in 25 people experienced domestic abuse in the year ending March 2023

Source: Crime Survey for England and Wales (CSEW) from the Office for National Statistics

Figure 2:

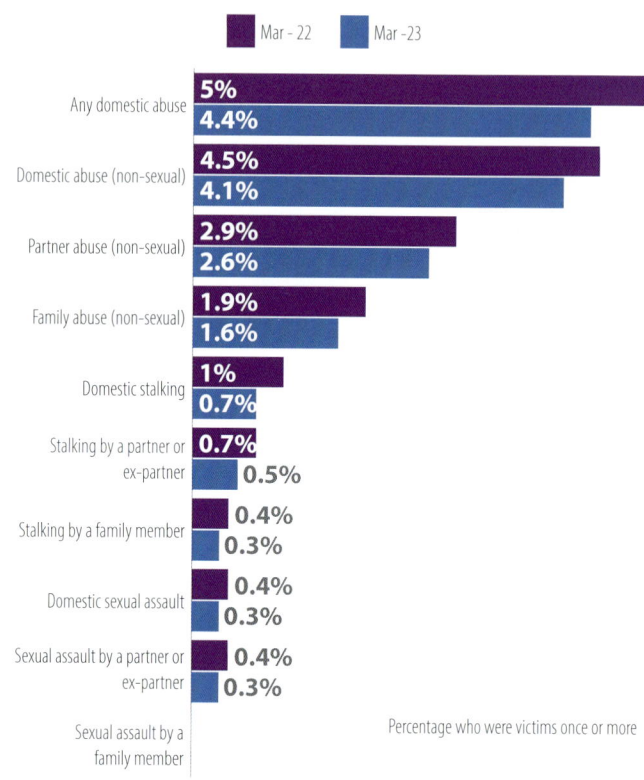

There were no statistically significant differences across domestic abuse types compared with the year ending March 2022

Prevalence of domestic abuse in the last year for people aged 16 years and over, by type of abuse, England and Wales, year ending March 2022 to year ending March 2023

Source: Crime Survey for England and Wales (CSEW) from the Office for National Statistics

- Have, or there has been a time when they each have had, a parental relationship in relation to the same child

The Domestic Abuse Act 2021 outlines the following behaviours as abuse:

- Physical or sexual abuse
- Violent or threatening behaviour
- Controlling or coercive behaviour
- Economic abuse
- Psychological, emotional, or other abuse

The Domestic Abuse Act 2021 recognises children under the age of 18 years who see, or hear, or experience the effects of the abuse, as a victim of domestic abuse if they are related or have a parental relationship to the adult victim or perpetrator of the abuse.

Domestic abuse in the last year

The CSEW estimated 2.1 million people aged 16 years and over experienced domestic abuse in the year ending March 2023, equating to a prevalence rate of 4.4%. The latest prevalence estimates for all types of domestic abuse experienced in the last year for people aged 16 years and over were not significantly different compared with the year ending March 2022.

Figure 1 shows a higher percentage of people aged 16 years and over experienced domestic abuse by a partner or ex-partner (3.0%) compared with a family member (1.8%) in the last year.

In the year ending March 2023, non-sexual domestic abuse was experienced by 4.1% of people aged 16 years and over compared with 4.5% in the previous year (Figure 2). Domestic stalking was experienced by 0.7% of people and domestic sexual assault was experienced by 0.3% of people in the last year, compared with 1.0% and 0.4% respectively, in the year ending March 2022. Differences seen for all types of abuse in the last year for people aged 16 and over, compared with the year ending March 2022, were not statistically significant.

Domestic abuse since the age of 16 years

The year ending March 2023, CSEW showed that an estimated 9.8 million people aged 16 years and over had experienced domestic abuse since the age of 16 years. This equates to a prevalence rate of approximately one in five people aged 16 years and over (Figure 4).

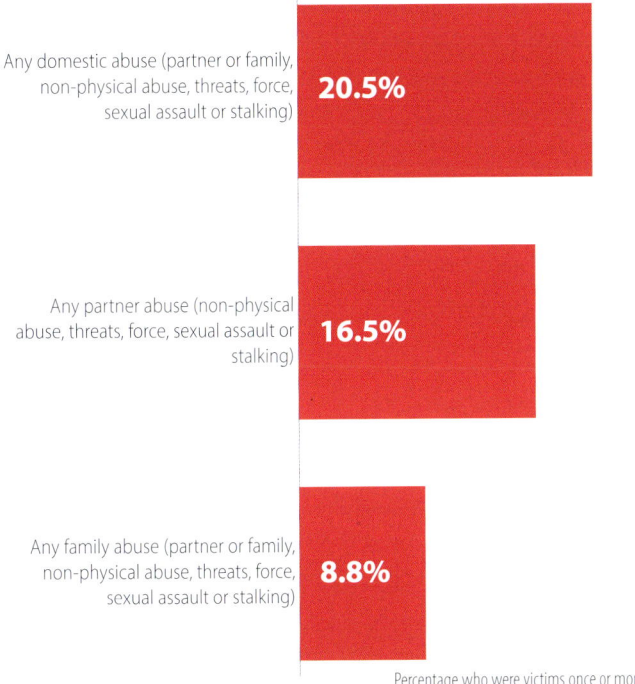

Figure 4:
Approximately one in five people had experienced domestic abuse since the age of 16 years

Source: Crime Survey for England and Wales (CSEW) from the Office for National Statistics

Figure 5 shows that non-sexual domestic abuse was experienced by 18.3% of people since the age of 16 years in the year ending March 2023. Around 14.0% of victims experienced non-sexual domestic abuse by a partner or ex-partner and 7.0% experienced non-sexual domestic abuse by a family member since the age of 16 years.

Controlling or coercive behaviour

There were 43,774 offences of coercive control recorded by the police in England and Wales (excluding Devon and Cornwall) in the year ending March 2023. This is compared with 41,039 in the year ending March 2022. The rise in coercive

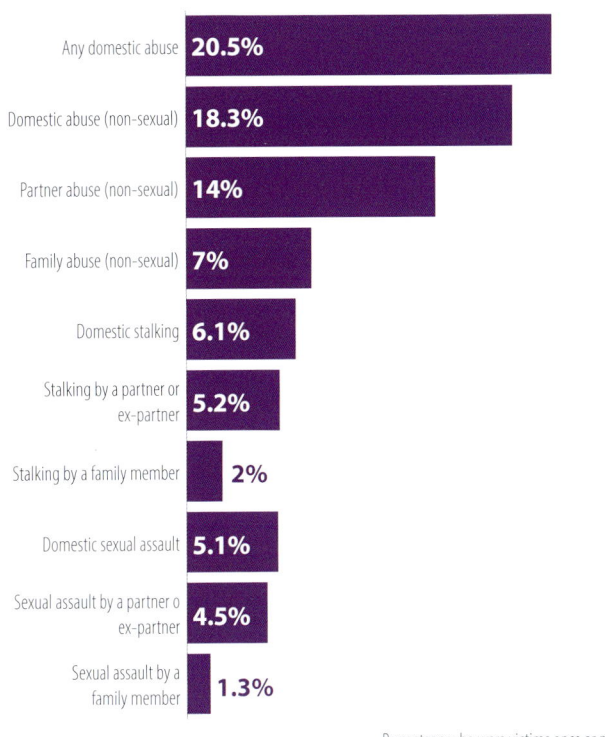

Figure 5:
Non-sexual domestic abuse was experienced by 18.3% of people since the age of 16 years

Prevalence of domestic abuse since the age of 16 years for people aged 16 years and over, by type of abuse, England and Wales, year ending March 2023

Source: Crime Survey for England and Wales (CSEW) from the Office for National Statistics

control offences over recent years may be attributed to improvements made by the police in recognising incidents of coercive control and using the new law accordingly.

Domestic homicide

Analysis on data from the Home Office Homicide Index combines data for a three-year period to account for the year-to-year variability in the volume of homicides.

There were 370 domestic homicides recorded by the police in the three-year period between year ending March 2020 and year ending March 2022. This represents approximately one in five of all homicides where the victim was aged 16 years and over during this period.

24 November 2023

The above information is reprinted with kind permission from the Office for National Statistics.
© Crown Copyright 2024
This information is licensed under the Open Government Licence v3.0
To view this licence, visit http://www.nationalarchives.gov.uk/doc/open-government-licence/

www.ons.gov.uk

Men can be victims of domestic abuse too

Men can be victims of domestic abuse too. Domestic violence does not discriminate based on gender and it's important to recognise that anyone, regardless of their sex, can experience physical, emotional, or psychological abuse within a relationship. Breaking down stereotypes and providing support for male victims is essential in addressing this issue and ensuring that all individuals have access to the help and resources they need to escape abusive situations and heal.

In the year ending March 2022, the police recorded 1,500,369 domestic abuse-related incidents and crimes in England and Wales.

The Crime Survey for England and Wales (CSEW) estimated 2.4 million adults aged 16 years and over experienced domestic abuse in the year ending March 2022 (1.7 million women and 699,000 men; 29% of all cases are men as the victim). This equates to a prevalence rate of approximately 5.0% of adults (6.9% women and 3.0% men).

Domestic abuse is not limited to physical violence and can include a range of abusive behaviours. It can also be experienced as repeated patterns of abusive behaviour to maintain power and control in a relationship.

The Domestic Abuse Act 2021 defines domestic abuse as any incident or pattern of incidents between those aged 16 years and over who:

- Are a partner
- Are an ex-partner
- Are a relative
- Have, or there has been a time when they each have had, a parental relationship in relation to the same child

The Domestic Abuse Act 2021 outlines the following behaviours as abuse:

- Physical or sexual abuse
- Violent or threatening behaviour
- Controlling or coercive behaviour
- Economic abuse
- Psychological, emotional, or other abuse

The Domestic Abuse Act 2021 recognises children under the age of 18 years who see, or hear, or experience the effects of the abuse, as a victim of domestic abuse if they are related or have a parental relationship to the adult victim or perpetrator of the abuse.

The Office for National Statistics figures show every year that one in the three victims of domestic abuse are male equating to approximately 757,000 men. This is a significant problem that often goes unrecognised and unreported. Did you know that one in six to seven men and one in 4 women will be a victim of domestic abuse in their lifetime?

This is evidence that every case of domestic abuse, for both males and females, should be taken seriously and each individual given access to the support they need.

Domestic abuse is not just limited to physical violence. It can also take the form of emotional, psychological and financial abuse. Men who experience domestic abuse may be subjected to verbal insults, threats, and manipulation. They may also have their money or property taken from them without their consent.

The effects of domestic abuse on men can be devastating. They may suffer from depression, anxiety, and other mental health issues as a result of the abuse. They may also experience physical injuries, such as bruises and broken bones. In extreme cases, domestic abuse can even lead to death.

One of the reasons that domestic abuse against men is often overlooked is because of attitudes and stereotypes about masculinity. Men are often expected to be strong and independent, and seeking help for domestic abuse may be seen as a sign of weakness. This can make it difficult for men to speak out about their experiences and get the help they need.

It is important to recognise that domestic abuse can happen to anyone, regardless of gender. Men who are experiencing domestic abuse should not be ashamed to seek help.

It is also crucial to raise awareness about domestic abuse against men. By educating people about the issue and encouraging victims to speak out, we can help to reduce the stigma and make it easier for men to get the help they need.

There are many organisations and support groups that can provide assistance and support to men who are in abusive situations.

On our 17 August 2022 virtual meeting, 'For Men To Talk' invited back 'The Paul Lavelle Foundation' for the first time since November 2020 to give us a presentation. Named after Paul Lavelle, who tragically passed away from a domestic abuse incident in 2017, the charity was created to raise awareness of male domestic abuse, support male victims and survivors and provide healthy relationship education as a preventative measure.

Due to the gap in service for support for males experiencing domestic abuse, the response to the Foundation grew considerably. Their office was opened in February 2019 by Barbara Lavelle and Neville Southall, ex-Everton goalkeeper and has grown from strength to strength ever since.

We know that domestic abuse is a serious problem that affects men as well as women. It is important to recognise that men can be victims of domestic abuse and to provide support and assistance to those who are in need. By raising awareness and providing support, we can help to reduce the incidence of domestic abuse and improve the lives of those who have been affected by it.

2023

Key Facts

- 2.4 million adults aged 16 years and over experienced domestic abuse in the year ending March 2022. 29% were men.
- 1 in 3 domestic abuse victims are male.
- 1 in 6-7 men and 1 in 4 women will be a victim of abuse in their iifetime.

Consider...

In small groups, discuss some of the stereotypes about men and masculinity and how they might prevent men from reporting domestic abuse.

Design

Design a poster to create awareness for male victims of domestic abuse.

Research

Can you find any stories in the media that discuss male victims of domestic abuse?

The above information is reprinted with kind permission from For Men To Talk.
© 2024 For Men To Talk

www.formentotalk.co.uk

Demand for men's domestic abuse helpline almost triples over 5 years

By Martha McHardy

Demand for the UK men's domestic abuse helpline has almost tripled since 2017, according to data obtained in a Freedom of Information request by *South West Londoner*.

The Men's Advice Line, a government-funded helpline for male victims of domestic abuse, has experienced a 170% increase in calls and emails since 2017.

In 2017–18, the helpline received 12,559 calls and 2,129 emails. However, the service has experienced a growth in demand since then, and in 2021–22 the helpline received 32,891 calls and 6,805 emails.

The data also shows the helpline experienced a 'rapid growth' in demand during the pandemic. There was a 41% increase in the number of calls and emails received during 2020–21.

Helpline Manager Tanisha Jnagel said: 'During the pandemic we saw rapid growth in demand across the Men's Advice Line. Male victims were locked down at home with their abusers, and isolated from their support networks.

'For many, this meant an increase in the frequency and severity of abuse, which resulted in an unprecedented 41% increase in demand for the helpline.'

During 2020–21, while the country was locked down, the helpline received 31,711 calls and 7,178 emails, up from 23,121 and 4,460 respectively the previous year.

The Men's Advice Line, which is funded by the Home Office, the Scottish Government, Scottish Women's Aid and London Councils, offers advice and emotional support to men who experience abuse, and signpost to other vital services that help men keep themselves and their children safe.

Since the pandemic, demand for the service has continued to grow.

Jnagel said: 'In 2021–22 we expected demand to decrease and return to more normal levels, but instead it has continued to grow, albeit at a slower rate.'

The Helpline Manager said the cost-of-living crisis has introduced new pressures and tensions into homes.

'Callers frequently discuss the ongoing impact of the pandemic on their relationships, and male victims are now experiencing the added pressures of the cost-of-living crisis. This is why demand has never returned to its pre-pandemic levels,' Jnagel said.

However, during 2021–22, the rate of growth of calls and emails to the helpline slowed, only increasing by 2% overall from the previous year, and the service experienced a 5% decrease in the number of emails.

Jnagel said men experience unique barriers when it comes to talking about their experiences of domestic abuse and reaching out for support.

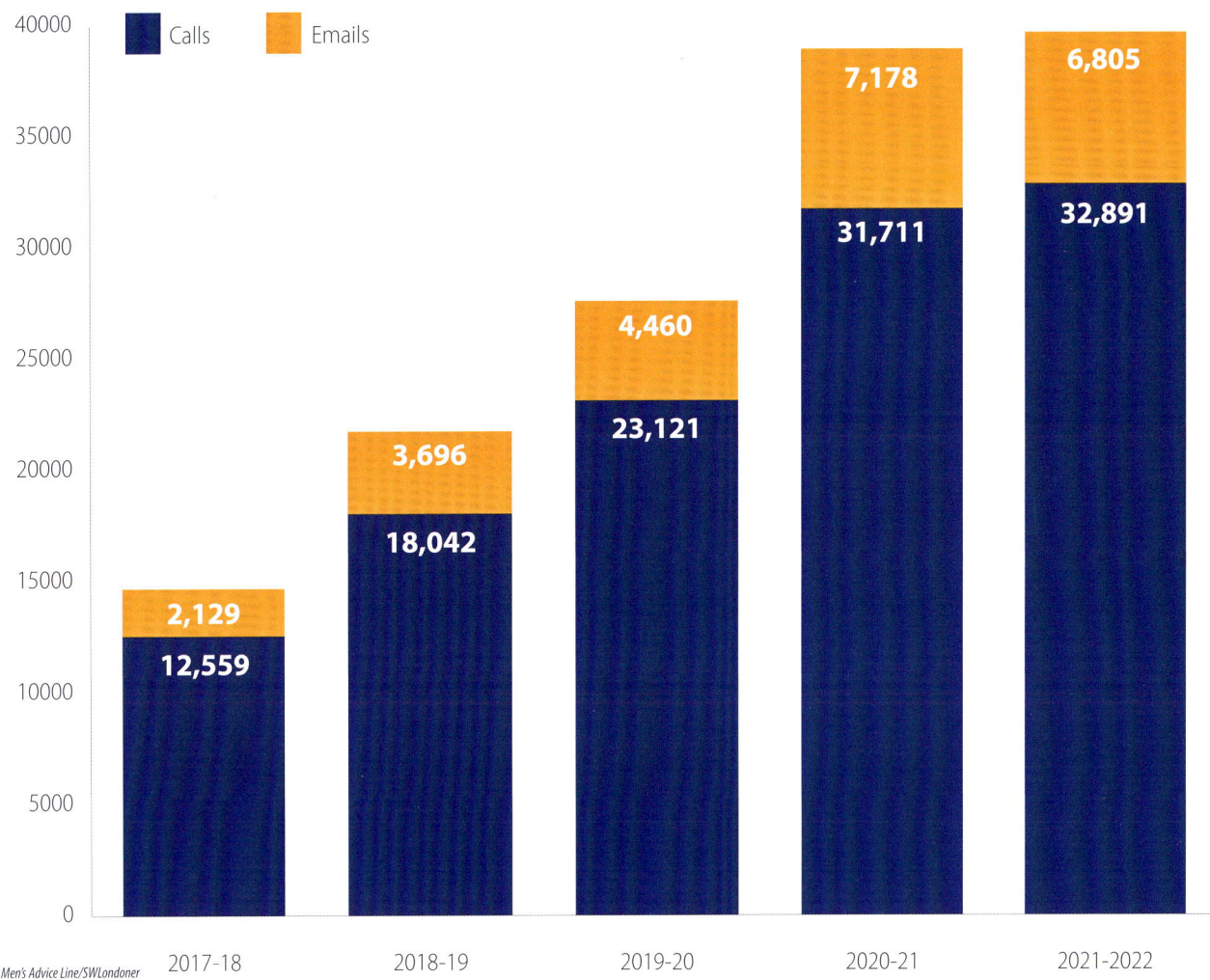

'There are barriers for all survivors of abuse when it comes to disclosing their experiences and reaching out for support. For all survivors, there can be a sense of shame, and a fear that they will be further harmed or separated from their children if they seek help or try to leave.

'Some barriers are unique to male victims, including a lack of awareness that men can be victims of abuse, and an embarrassment that they, as a man, have been victimised.

'Another key barrier we're hearing about at the moment is concern around the financial impact of leaving an abusive partner.

'This is the same for survivor services supporting women, but we often hear from men that they worry they cannot afford to flee and rebuild their own lives, whilst still financially supporting their family.'

Jnagel stressed that male victims should call the helpline for confidential support, regardless of whether they are in a straight or gay relationship.

'Men can experience domestic abuse too. It doesn't make you less of a man, and it doesn't say anything about your strength or your character. Reach out for support so you can live a life free from violence and abuse,' said Jnagel.

If you are a man who has experienced domestic abuse, or you know a man who has, call the Men's Advice Line on 0808 8010327.

15 January 2023

Key Facts

- During 2020–21, while the country was locked down, the helpline received 31,711 calls and 7,178 emails, up from 23,121 and 4,460 respectively the previous year.

Design

Design a poster for the Men's Advice Line. Make sure that you display all of their contact information.

The above information is reprinted with kind permission from South West Londoner.
© 1997-2024 South West Londoner

www.swlondoner.co.uk

Helping male victims of domestic abuse can benefit society as a whole

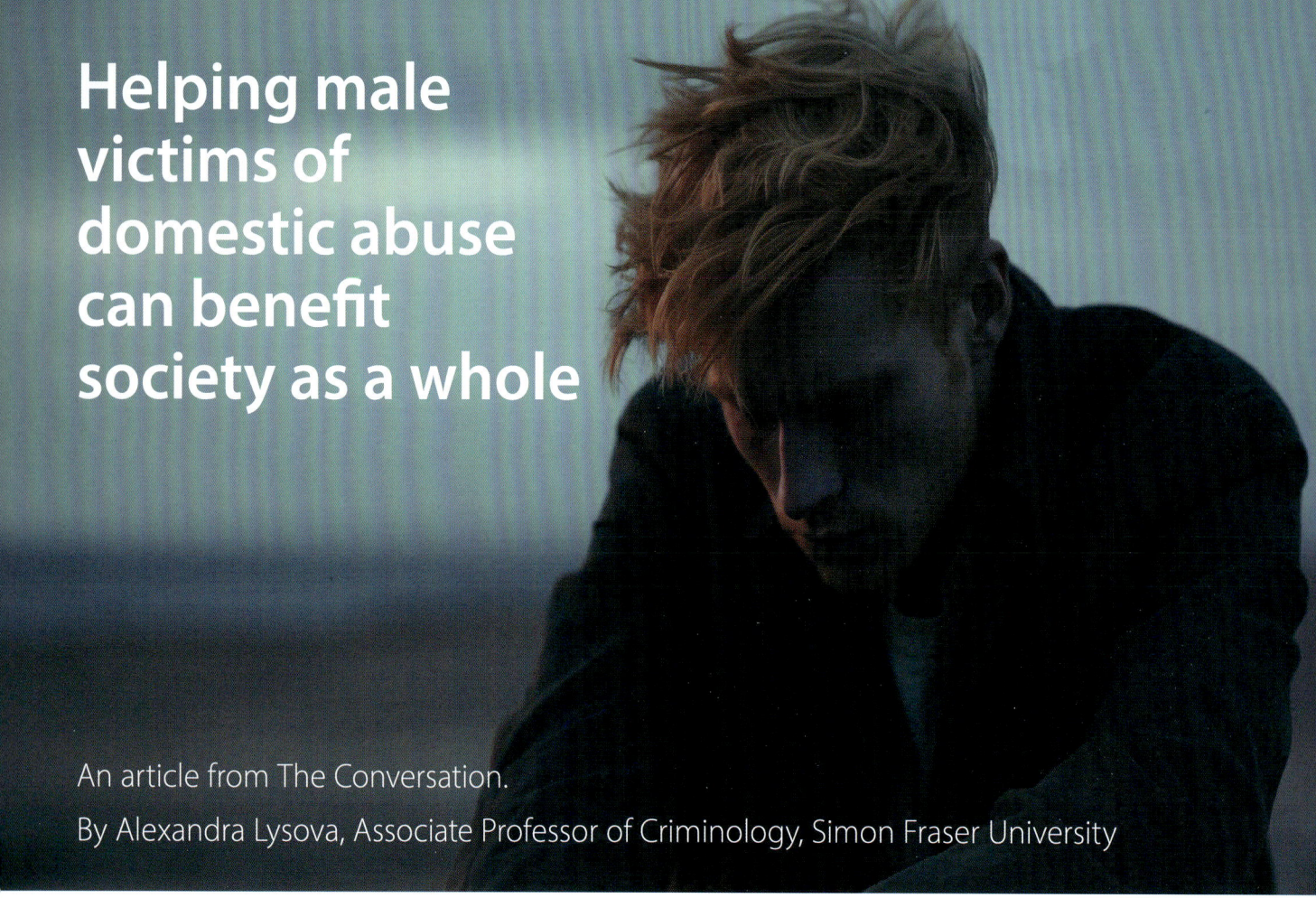

An article from The Conversation.

By Alexandra Lysova, Associate Professor of Criminology, Simon Fraser University

Every year in early December, the UN holds its 16 Days of Activism against Gender-Based Violence. The issue is one that can affect everyone regardless of their sex, gender or gender identity.

However, men who experience violence, and efforts to prevent violence against men and boys, are conspicuously lacking from the gender-based violence discussion. Despite solid evidence of men's experiences of violent victimization in Canada, the U.S. and elsewhere, services for them are virtually non-existent.

I have been studying men's intimate partner victimization and domestic violence more generally for over 15 years. I believe that helping male victims of intimate partner abuse will also address violence against women and girls by breaking the cycle of violence, and will benefit society as a whole.

Men as victims of intimate partner violence

Men are overrepresented among victims of homicide and suicide. Research on intimate partner violence – recently highlighted by the *Johnny Depp v. Amber Heard* case – suggests that men can also become victims of female-perpetrated partner violence.

Self-reported population studies – one of the major sources of data on partner violence – identified that one in five men (19.3 per cent) in North America and western Europe experience physical violence in an intimate relationship annually.

In Canada, about 655,000 men reported having experienced physical victimization in intimate relationships between 2004 and 2014. Moreover, about 64,000 of these men experienced the most severe type of partner abuse characterized by repeated and severe physical and psychological violence with a high probability of injuries and negative emotional effects.

A U.S study found that people in same-sex relationships can experience higher levels of domestic violence. Just over half (55 per cent) of police-reported same-sex partner violence in Canada involved male partners. These individuals may face special barriers when it comes to discussing their experiences or seeking help.

We are also learning that men are at a higher risk of experiencing legal and administrative abuse in the intimate relationships, including false accusations of abuse. A 2020 survey found that 11 per cent of American men reported being falsely accused of domestic violence or other forms of abuse.

The second major source of data – police-reported statistics – indicates that women are more likely to experience the most severe injurious violence and intimate partner homicide. Police-reported data also reveals that women and girls make up almost 70 per cent of family-violence victims in Canada. There are however limitations on police-reported data. For example, about 80 per cent of victims of abuse never report it to the police, and men tend to underreport spousal violence compared to women.

Despite under reporting, police data identified concerning trends of family violence for male victims. Between 2009 and 2021, the rates of police-reported family-violence in Canada decreased by five per cent for women and girls but increased by four per cent for men and boys.

Gap in services for men

Like other victims, men require attention and help with recognizing abuse earlier so they can cope with the consequences of abuse more effectively.

An international study I was a part of in 2020 found gender-specific barriers to men seeking help, including not recognizing or calling what happened to them abuse, trying to live up to notions of 'manliness' (being a victim may be seen as unmanly), trying to fix the relationship, protecting children and simply because they had nowhere to go for help.

There is a drastic service gap for male victims of abuse compared to female victims of partner abuse. Among 557 government-funded residential facilities for victims of crime in Canada, only 24 reported being mandated to also serve men in addition to women.

Breaking the cycle of violence

Adults are not the only victims of domestic abuse. Children's exposure to domestic violence – when children witness a parent assault another parent or partner – is a widespread social problem.

Around 25 per cent of youth in the U.S. are affected by it in their lifetime. Children of men who are victimized by their female partners often witness the violence and/or experience direct physical and emotional abuse.

Preventing violence by any partner can help to break the cycle of violence – or what is known as the intergenerational transmission of violence. That is when children who witness or experience abuse are more likely to engage in violent partner relationships in adulthood.

Moreover, boys are much more likely than girls to experience physical childhood abuse, including being kicked, bitten, punched, choked, burned or otherwise attacked. Eliminating this type of abuse could reduce men's perpetration of violence against women and children in their future relationship.

Many people might think that most intimate partner violence is perpetrated only by men and directed toward women. However, the most common pattern of abuse is bidirectional violence. That is, violence perpetrated and experienced by both people in a relationship. Around 58 per cent of reported cases of intimate partner violence were bidirectional.

The impact of the bidirectional violence can be very serious, including physical injury and mental health problems for both partners. Recognizing and addressing partner violence that involves mutually violent couples can reduce violence against both men and women.

Helping men means saving lives

Strong evidence suggests that helping male victims of domestic violence can help reduce the likelihood of homicide for both men and women. In the U.S. and Canada, research has shown that when abused women are able to leave violent relationships, like finding refuge in a shelter for abused women, there is a reduction in female-perpetrated homicides.

If abused men had similar opportunities to receive timely help, it could prevent abusive relationships from escalating, and potentially reduce male-perpetrated homicides as well as the deaths of men who are killed by their partners.

It is time to recognize men's experiences of violence and abuse, not only as perpetrators but also as victims. Engaging men in reducing gender-based violence against women is important, but not enough.

Helping men and boys prevent violence in their own lives and providing them with support to address the consequences of partner abuse is the next important step in eliminating intimate partner violence.

22 December 2022

Key Facts

- One in five men (19.3 per cent) in North America and western Europe experience physical violence in an intimate relationship annually.

- In Canada, about 655,000 men reported having experienced physical victimization in intimate relationships between 2004 and 2014.

- A U.S study found that people in same-sex relationships can experience higher levels of domestic violence.

- Just over half (55 per cent) of police-reported same-sex partner violence in Canada involved male partner.

- Women are more likely to experience the most severe injurious violence and intimate partner homicide.

THE CONVERSATION

The above information is reprinted with kind permission from The Conversation.
© 2010-2024, The Conversation Trust (UK) Limited

www.theconversation.com

You were told: a voice for killed women

An extract.

By Anna Ryder and Jhiselle Feanny

This report is based on the testimony and experiences of bereaved families who have lost loved ones to violence. It contains content that some may find traumatic.

Introduction and context

A woman is killed by a man every three days in the UK. 62% of these women are killed by partners or ex-partners and 70% are killed in the sanctuary of their home. These murders are brutal and cruel; in over half of them there is evidence of 'overkill' – the use of 'excessive, gratuitous violence beyond that which is necessary to cause death', and many are killed in front of their children.

As harrowing as these statistics are, they do not convey the enormity of the impact of these crimes and the deep-rooted culture of inequality and misogyny which enables them. They do not convey the deep lifelong suffering inflicted on the families torn apart, or the violence, rapes and abuse suffered by many victims before their death. They do not express the threat of danger many women and girls feel forced to navigate every day.

It is in the voices of the families who have lost loved ones that we hear and come to understand what lies beneath the numbers. That is why a year ago, we set up Killed Women – a campaigning organisation led by and representing the families of victims of fatal male violence, to unite and lend these powerful voices to ending Violence Against Women and Girls (VAWG). We have three strategic aims:

1. To bring an end to fatal male violence against women in the UK and to tackle the culture of violence that enables it.
2. To ensure justice for victims and their families.
3. To improve the rights and provision of support for families who have lost loved ones to male violence, particularly for children.

Survey participants

A total of 115 respondents took part in the survey.

Base: Relatives of killed women (115). Answer options with base sizes of less than 10 have been removed or combined to maintain participant confidentiality
Source: Killed Women

A wide range of family members came forward to complete the survey including fathers, sons, brothers, nieces, aunts, uncles, cousins and grandmothers of victims, but the biggest groups of respondents were sisters (30%), mothers (16%) and daughters (13%). Just over half (51%) of respondents reported that the perpetrator was the partner, husband or boyfriend of the victim; 25% reported that the perpetrator was the ex-partner, husband or boyfriend, and 8% reported a male relative of some kind. In 10% of cases the perpetrator was a stranger, in 7% a colleague.

The majority of respondents (76%) said that the perpetrators were convicted for murder, while 16% were convicted for manslaughter. Nearly all cases involved a single perpetrator, with 97% of relatives stating this. Most of the women killed were aged between 16–44 years (77%). Many had children under the age of 18 at the time of their death (45%). In 96% of responses, the victim referred to was a UK citizen.

Around one in five (17%) respondents said the victims had at least one complex need such as homelessness, mental health challenges, or addiction or substance dependency and 7% said the victims experienced so-called 'honour-based' abuse and violence.

Most of the cases reported in this survey (69%), are recent, occurring between 2010 and 2022, but some cases dated back as far as the 1970s. It was possible for different relatives of the women who had been killed to participate in the survey. Due to the confidential nature of the survey it is not possible to say how many different killed women are represented.

You were told

Only 4% of respondents felt their loved one's death was 'not preventable at all', with 67% saying it was 'very' or 'fairly' preventable'. This section of the report expands on why families felt this way. It also details the services and agencies that were alerted to abuse suffered by victims before they were killed, and how families rated their response.

Respondents felt homicides were preventable

4% of respondents thought the death of their loved one was 'not preventable at all', while shockingly 67% thought the homicide was 'very preventable' or 'fairly preventable.' Those who felt that the homicide was preventable were asked for more details on how they thought these crimes may have been stopped.

Knowledge of prior abuse towards victim not acted upon

Respondents believed their loved ones' death could have been prevented if the services or agencies that had prior knowledge of the abuse suffered by the victim had done more. Among those who stated there was a history of abuse, an alarming 78% said one or more services knew about this abuse and 69% said two or more services knew; this included the police, GPs, schools, legal services, social services and the Crown Prosecution Service. The majority of references were made to the failure of the police to take appropriate steps to protect their loved one. Comments from respondents included:

- *The police failed her. They did not give her support and listen to the urgency in her needs. Police and hospital both could have done so much more. She would have had a chance at life.*
- *The school was told of the abuse by her children but did not take appropriate action. The authorities were aware and did not communicate with other authorities... Health visitors were too afraid to attend the house due to fear of the perpetrator...*
- *Police took no action despite several written and verbal threats to kill my sister.*

Histories of perpetrators not acted on

Two-thirds (65%) of respondents said the perpetrator had a history of criminality, violence, or abusive behaviour. Of those, 59% said the perpetrator had a history of being violent or abusive towards other women. When asked to expand on their experience, respondents believed that not only should this history have resulted in further action from authorities at an earlier stage, but that they, as family members, should have been informed about it.

- *We didn't know about Clare's Law until it was too late.*
- *The perpetrator had a conviction history of abuse to ex-partner and others.*
- *There are decades of evidence that show that VAWG are serial and escalating offences. This perpetrator was condoned and enabled by the state that dismisses VAWG until the point of murder. He should have been stopped after the first offences.*

In some cases, the perpetrator had killed before.

- *...The monster had killed before... he had a colourful past of violence towards women, and this was known to all services but not us as a family.*
- *He was on probation life licence for a previous murder. They didn't monitor him properly or drug test him.*

Which, of the following organisations or services, if any, knew about the perpetrators abuse towards your relative, prior to her death?

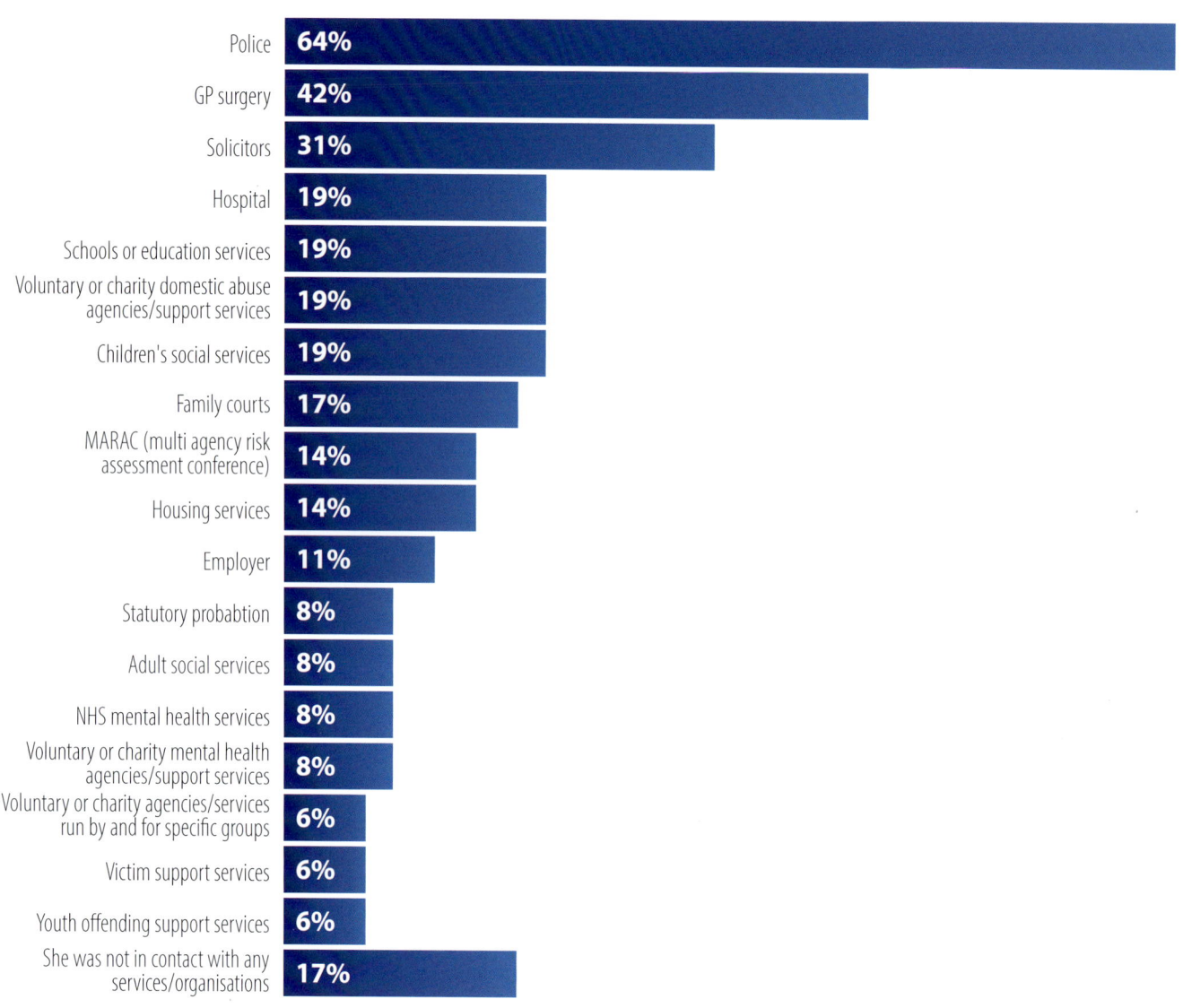

Base: Respondents who's relative had previously experienced abuse or violence by the perpetrator (36).
Source: Killed Women

Families mentioned several other issues including employers not doing enough to ensure the victim's safety at work; concerns about the perpetrator's mental health or substance abuse not being acted upon; or the criminal justice system's failure to pursue cases without the victim's consent.

Others believed perpetrators were able to access dangerous weapons too easily through a gun licence.

- *He should never have been given a gun licence... If he didn't have the gun there could have been a very different outcome.*
- *The killer was given a gun licence and able to buy a gun, even though he had a history of depression, lied on his form, lied to the police and the doctor did not raise concern.*

A lack of education or understanding of misogyny, stalking, harassment or coercive control was also mentioned, as respondents felt neither they nor their relative had been taught to identify dangerous behaviours in perpetrators. One respondent said:

- *(I believe the perpetrator) was coercively controlling to previous girlfriends and stalked them. I believe if this behaviour was talked about in schools more and the danger these individuals pose when they end a relationship, [my relative] would never have dated him.*

Services knew about abuse prior to homicide and responded poorly

Prior abuse suffered by victims was known about by services

Where relatives said they were aware victims had suffered previous abuse from the perpetrator, survey respondents were asked which services or agencies were alerted of the abuse their loved one was suffering.

Two-thirds (64%) of respondents whose relative had previously experienced abuse by the perpetrator said that this abuse was reported to the police.

The survey also revealed that other services were alerted to the abuse, most commonly GP surgeries (42%) and solicitors (31%).

The survey findings also suggest that multiple services knew of the abuse the victims were experiencing, with 69%

of respondents whose relative had previously experienced abuse by the perpetrator, mentioning two or more services who knew about the abuse, and 50% stating three or more.

- *No one joined the dots. Everyone that knew what was happening just heard the information and did nothing.*

- *She reported threats to kill five times, and one rape report to police, as well as one attempt to kill her. They were very dismissive and racist. School knew about it from previous family reports… Social Services knew about it… There were so many failings from Social Services. Hospital knew about it from the attempt to kill after she attended there for treatment due to her injuries. Police attended and failed once again to support her and keep her safe.*

Services responded poorly to known abuse

Many of these respondents felt that the services and agencies alerted to the abuse responded poorly, missing critical opportunities to help their loved one before it was too late. Of the respondents who stated that the police knew about abuse prior to the homicide, 78% (n=18) thought that police performance was 'fairly poor' or 'very poor'. Alarmingly, no-one considered the police's performance as 'very good.' When asked to expand, several respondents discussed how the police knew about the abuse being suffered but did not act, seeming to fail to take what was happening seriously enough.

- *She had made complaints to the police before; they knew he was dangerous, but they failed to act. It was always so difficult to get them to take it seriously even though she suffered being beaten up, and emotional abuse.*

- *The police were useless. They actually admitted he would have to kill her before they could do anything.*

The ratings given to other services and agencies were equally concerning. All of the respondents who stated that children services knew about previous abuse (n=7) rated the response as 'very poor' or 'fairly poor,' and 80% (n=12 of 15) of applicable respondents rated GPs' response as 'very poor' or 'fairly poor.'

Furthermore, several respondents expressed frustration at how the services did not share knowledge of the abuse being suffered with each other.

- *The services did not discuss their concerns with other services, they dismissed the abuse as not being severe enough.*

One respondent highlighted how this impacted the victim's ability to prove the risk the perpetrator posed.

- *None of the agencies shared the data/evidence of abuse and the impact of abuse on (my relative)…either with her, or with other agencies. Which meant, when (she) tried to prove to the courts (that) he was an abusive man, it was literally her word against his…*

Some respondents also commented on the victim's race or cultural background affecting service or agencies response:

- *(She) completely gave up on the system she now saw as being both deeply sexist and racist.*

5 December 2023

Key Facts

- A woman is killed by a man every three days in the UK.
- 62% of these women are killed by partners or ex-partners and 70% are killed in the sanctuary of their home.
- Over half of these deaths have the use of 'excessive, gratuitous violence beyond that which is necessary to cause death.'
- Most of the women killed were aged between 16–44 years (77%).

The above information is reprinted with kind permission from Killed Women.
© 2024 Killed Women

www.killedwomen.org

Domestic abusers who kill their partners to face tougher sentences

Campaigners highlighted the case of Poppy Waterhouse, 24, whose ex-boyfriend inflicted more than 100 injuries but was jailed for just 16 years.

By Charles Hymas

Domestic abusers who kill their partners face a minimum of 25 years in jail under plans to end 'soft' sentences for domestic homicide.

Ministers are proposing a shake-up under which killers with a history of coercive or controlling behaviour against their victims will face tougher sentences.

The use of excessive or gratuitous violence will also be made an aggravating factor in sentencing decisions for murder, the Ministry of Justice (MoJ) announced.

The changes to the law follow a review by Clare Wade, King's Counsel (KC), who was defence barrister for Sally Challen, the first woman to have her conviction for murdering her husband quashed under coercive control laws.

Ms Wade found that the current sentencing system failed to take account of the fact that many domestic homicides are preceded by years of abuse.

Justice Secretary Dominic Raab said: 'This government will do everything we can to protect vulnerable women and keep in prison for longer those who attack or threaten them.'

Higher sentencing of 25 years minimum discussed

The MoJ will consult on whether there should be a higher sentencing starting point of 25 years for murder cases where the perpetrator has a history of controlling and coercive abuse.

The 25-year minimum currently only applies to premeditated killings where a knife is taken to the scene of the crime. That is 10 years more than the current starting point for murder in the home where a weapon, such as a kitchen knife, may already be present.

Under the changes, judges will also be required to treat coercive or controlling behaviour by a killer as an 'aggravating' factor which means they are expected to increase the sentence. The same will apply to so-called 'overkill' offences where a killer causes multiple injuries in a frenzy of violence and anger.

The government has also asked the Sentencing Council to review guidelines for manslaughter to ensure cases where deaths occur during rough sex should be punished with longer jail terms.

Although the law is clear that there is no such thing as a 'rough sex defence', the review found that the high risk of death these acts may carry should be reflected in sentences potentially several years longer.

Campaigners have highlighted cases such as Poppy Waterhouse, 24, who was murdered by her ex-boyfriend in a drunken attack fuelled by jealousy and rage. He stabbed her to death with a knife from their kitchen, inflicting more than 100 injuries but was jailed for just 16 years.

Around one in four (26%) homicides in England and Wales are committed by a current or former partner or relative.

Of the murder cases reviewed by Clare Wade over half (51%) involved controlling or coercive behaviour while excessive violence, or overkill, was identified in 60%, with men being the perpetrator in all but one case.

Carole Gould and Julie Devey, who co-founded the campaigning organisation Killed Women after the deaths of their daughters, welcomed the government moves but said: 'They must be just the start of the root-and-branch reform that is needed to ensure killers of women face sentences that reflect the cruelty and brutality of their crimes.'

The pair called on the government to make sure the changes 'are felt in courtrooms.'

Vera Baird, the former victims' commissioner, said the MoJ needed to take action on Ms Wade's proposals to take account of the female victims of abuse who subsequently kill.

'Making the use of controlling and coercive behaviour an aggravating factor for perpetrators who kill, while failing to make it a mitigating factor for women who kill only through having been victims of it, is to do injustice to those women,' she said.

Domestic homicide is defined as a death that occurs due to violence, abuse, or neglect by a partner, ex-partner, relative or member of the same household.

Controlling or coercive behaviour was introduced as a criminal offence in the Serious Crime Act 2015 and can include economic, emotional, or psychological abuse and threats alongside physical or sexual violence.

Women victims of coercive control should have shorter sentences for killings

Women who have been victims of coercive control should have shorter sentences if they kill their abusive partners, a government review has recommended.

The review for the MoJ said that courts should take account of coercive control as a potential 'mitigating' factor in domestic homicide.

It also said judges should consider taking account of the lower culpability for a killing if they had been victims of coercive control, which under sentencing guidelines would mean a shorter prison term.

They are among a series of recommendations that are being considered by the government under the review by Clare Wade, KC, the defence barrister for Sally Challen, the first woman to have her conviction for murdering her husband quashed under coercive control laws.

Last week the government confirmed that it would increase the sentences for killers who had subjected their victims to years of domestic abuse and coercive control. It will mean domestic abusers who kill their partners face a minimum of 25 years in jail.

However, ministers held back from making any change in the rules for victims of domestic abuse who kill their partners despite calls from women's groups to do so. A decision on these recommendations is unlikely until the Summer.

In her review, Ms Wade said: 'Research shows that when women are convicted of murdering their male partners, they often tend to be the victims of previous domestic abuse by their partners,

'Women who have suffered domestic abuse in a relationship which is governed by coercive control are likely to kill because the coercive control had led to such a degree of entrapment that they can see no other or lawful way out of their situation.'

Psychologists had identified the condition as 'perspecticide,' one of devastating isolation. 'In circumstances where such women are convicted of murder, research has shown that this is often because of failings in the criminal justice system,' said the review.

'Either, such women are not properly protected from previous domestic abuse or not properly represented at trial. Another reason we suggest that such women are often convicted of murder is that the dominant discourse is not yet one of coercive control, which, as we have already argued, underpins domestic abuse.'

The review recommended that where there was a history of coercive control it should be treated as 'an aggravating or mitigating factor.'

'Any policy which did not take account of the fact that a minority of perpetrators are also victims of the very mischief that the sentencing policy is designed to reflect/address would lead to injustice,' said the report.

It also recommended that infidelity should not be treated as a mitigating factor in domestic homicide.

17 March 2023

Key Facts
- Around one in four (26%) homicides in England and Wales are committed by a current or former partner or relative.

The above information is reprinted with kind permission from *The Telegraph*.
© Telegraph Media Group Limited 2023

www.telegraph.co.uk

Signs of Abuse

Chapter 2

I'm not sure if my relationship is healthy

Disagreements in relationships are normal but when they become frequent and begin to form a pattern, it might be a sign that something is wrong, and possibly abusive – a word that is hard for many people to think about or even say out loud.

Something doesn't feel right

If something doesn't feel right in your relationship, it probably isn't.

An abuser may say things like 'I didn't mean it,' 'I was having a bad day,' 'It only happened once' in order to justify or excuse their hurtful behaviour. This might make you start doubting whether your concerns about your relationship are valid. If you've heard any of these before, it could be a sign of an unhealthy or controlling relationship.

Another sign of an abusive relationship can be if your behaviour has changed because of how your partner treats you or your children. Perpetrators often create justifications for their actions, which they use to place blame on survivors and to take away any responsibility from themselves.

We're here to tell you that perpetrators alone are responsible for their actions. We're here to support you and help you to explore your options, because you deserve a kind, healthy relationship where you don't feel trapped.

A healthy relationship should be a loving, respectful place with values like support, freedom, happiness and consent at the centre.

How to recognise unhealthy behaviour in a relationship

Every situation is unique, but there are some common factors in relationships that might mean they are unhealthy and even abusive. Just thinking about these red-flag behaviours is an important first step. You've come to the right place to begin this journey.

Look through the examples on this page and the next that signal something is 'off' in a relationship, in some cases, it could signal abuse. The descriptions might feel a bit overwhelming at first glance and may be painful to acknowledge, but try to read as many as you can because it's important you know the unhealthy behaviours before they escalate further. If something doesn't feel right in your relationship, it probably isn't.

Physical abuse

Physical abuse is one of the first forms of domestic abuse that people recognise because it's the most visible. It is often a way for a perpetrator to gain control. It is illegal. Some examples of physical abuse are:

- Punching, slapping, hitting, pinching, kicking, scratching or biting
- Applying pressure to your neck or holding you down, strangling or choking you
- Pulling your hair out
- Spitting at you or near you
- Using objects as weapons to attack or hurt you
- Punching walls or breaking things.

Psychological and emotional abuse

Psychological and emotional abuse can be difficult to describe or identify. It's when a perpetrator uses words and non-physical actions to manipulate, hurt, scare, or upset you. Some examples of emotional and verbal abuse are:

- Screaming and shouting at you
- Mocking you, calling you hurtful names, or using derogatory words about you
- Sulking or refusing to talk or be kind until you do something they want

issues: Domestic Abuse

- Making you doubt your own sanity. This is known as gaslighting. A perpetrator may gaslight you into thinking that you are remembering things wrong or that you are misinterpreting things, later making you believe their version of events is true. This behaviour is often used to manipulate.
- Threatening that they will destroy something, hurt you or commit suicide
- Threatening to report you to the police, social services or a mental health team if you don't do what they say
- Telling you that they're sorry, that it isn't abuse
- Telling you that you deserve or cause the abuse
- Threatening to kill or harm you and/or your children.

Coercive control

Coercive control is an act or pattern of acts of assault, threats, humiliation and intimidation, which is used to harm, punish or frighten. Some examples of coercive control are:

- Isolating you from your friends and family
- Depriving you of basic needs, such as food or care
- Monitoring how you spend your time
- Tracking what you do online or on your phone
- Controlling aspects of your everyday life, such as where you can go, who you can see, what you can wear and when you can sleep
- Stopping you from accessing support services, such as medical services or support groups
- Repeatedly putting you down, saying you are worthless
- Humiliating, degrading or dehumanising you

Financial and economic abuse

Financial abuse is part of coercive control, it involves a pattern of controlling, threatening and degrading behaviours relating to money and finances. The perpetrator uses money to control their partner's freedom. This can include using credit or debit cards without permission or building up debts in their partner's name. Economic abuse is a broader term, as it also includes restricting access to essential resources and services, such as food, clothing or transport, and refusing to allow someone to improve their economic status through employment, education or training. Some examples of economic abuse are:

- Controlling all of the household income and keeping financial information a secret
- Taking out debts in your name, sometimes without you knowing
- Stopping you from being in work, education, or training
- Making you do a certain amount of hours at work, not contributing to any bills
- Having control over spending, checking receipts, having everything in their name.

Sexual abuse

Sexual abuse and violence can take place within relationships or between family members and can often be a part of domestic abuse. If you consent to something because you are afraid or you have been pressured into it, it is not consent. Some examples of sexual abuse are:

- Rape or sexual assault. This can be any sexual act you did not consent to. It can include forced kissing, touching or penetration. If you have experienced this recently, find advice on getting treatment and support on the Women's Aid website.
- Having sex with you when you are unable to consent, for example if you are under the influence of drugs or alcohol which may affect your ability to consent.
- Using force, threats, guilt, manipulation, or intimidation to make you perform sexual acts.
- Forcing you to have sex with other people or to become a sex worker.
- Forcing you to have sex or watch pornography in front of children.
- Degrading you during sex, such as calling you names, spitting, biting, punching, or hurting you.

Tech abuse

Tech abuse is when someone uses technology as a tool to abuse. As our homes become smarter, this type of abuse is becoming more common. Abusers may use smart home devices to monitor and control. This could include connecting to thermostats to change the temperature, turning lights or speakers on and off from an app, or watching you on security cameras. It can also include cyberstalking;, when someone repeatedly sends harassing messages.

Some examples of tech abuse are:

- Monitoring your social media
- Having access to your phone, email account, and/or social media accounts. You have a right to privacy.
- Having access to your online banking
- Not allowing you to have access to technology, such as a phone, or internet access
- Sharing intimate photos of you online. If you have experienced this type of abuse, the Revenge Porn Helpline can support you.
- Using cameras or spyware to watch you or listen to your conversations
- Using GPS locators or tracking apps on your phone to locate you
- Constantly contacting you through text, calls, email and/or social media
- Using smart home devices to harass you.

See page 37 for Asha's story

The above information is reprinted with kind permission from Women's Aid.
© 2024 Women's Aid
www.womensaid.org.uk

Love-bombing and gaslighting: tactics of domestic abuse

Love-bombing and gaslighting are two forms of emotional abuse and manipulation used by people in intimate relationships. Both are dangerous, damaging behaviours that can have long-lasting and negative effects on victims.

Love-bombing is a form of manipulation and psychological abuse where the abuser showers the victim with signs of affection, attention, and praise. It is a way to build an intense connection quickly and make the victim feel special, loved, and accepted. This form of manipulation is often used to cover up the abuser's intentions or to win over the victim's trust. The love-bomber will use compliments, gifts, sweet words, flattery, promises of a brighter future together, or other forms of affection to manipulate their partner into staying in the relationship. However, once the abuser has achieved their desired outcome they may suddenly turn cold or abusive.

Gaslighting is another form of emotional manipulation and abuse where the abuser attempts to make their victim doubt their own perceptions or memories by questioning reality. It's a subtle yet powerful form of psychological abuse that makes victims doubt themselves and feel confused about what is real or not. The abuser will often deny wrongdoing or accuse their partner of being crazy for believing something different from what they have said. For example, if an abuser says something like 'that never happened' when their partner remembers it happening differently, this is gaslighting. The goal is for the victim to become so confused that they start to believe what their abuser says instead of trusting themselves. Over time this can lead to feelings of insecurity, worthlessness, and even depression in victims who are constantly subjected to gaslighting tactics from their abusers.

When combined, love-bombing and gaslighting constitute domestic abuse because they both involve one person controlling another through emotional manipulation and psychological tactics such as lying or denial, which can be just as damaging as physical violence. Victims may feel confused about what is real or not due to gaslighting while also feeling dependent on their abuser due to love-bombing tactics which prevent them from leaving the relationship even when they know it's unhealthy for them. As such, these manipulative behaviours can be extremely damaging both mentally and emotionally for victims who are constantly subjected to them over time without realising it until it's too late.

It's important for people in relationships with potential abusers to be aware of these toxic behaviours so that they can recognise them before it becomes too late. If someone notices any signs that either love-bombing or gaslighting may be taking place in a relationship then it's important that they reach out for help immediately before things get worse as these manipulative tactics can have long-lasting effects on victims even after they manage to escape from an abusive situation.

28 February 2023

The above information is reprinted with kind permission from Right to Equality.
© 2024 Right to Equality

www.righttoequality.org

How to speak to your partner about gaslighting – and when to end the relationship

By Dayna McAlpine

'Look, you can't be mad at me for that, you're totally overreacting.'

Tom*, 27, from Manchester, had become used to this response when confronting his ex-partner over her behaviour towards him – a repetitive cycle where he somehow found himself being gaslit over questioning her gaslighting.

For those who aren't familiar with the dating term 'gaslighting', it's far from just a silly buzzword for a relationship trend – it's a pattern of toxic behaviour that can be incredibly damaging to those on the receiving end of it.

A major part of abusive relationships, gaslighting involves a person using relentless denial, lying, and contradiction to make someone else feel unsure of their own sanity and perception of situations.

It's not a toxic behaviour exclusive to just romantic relationships; you can find yourself being gaslit in friendships, by family, and even in the workplace.

'I was gaslit for years by my ex, who would constantly say things like "I thought you were confident", "you told me you were confident", "I find confidence attractive, who are you and where have you gone?"', shares Jenna*, 31, from Edinburgh.

'This drove me insane and made me question my identity and sense of self (and self-worth), plaguing my mind with thoughts like "Have I misled her about who I am?", "am I a disappointment?", "she's right".'

Sound familiar? Or maybe you're in a relationship (whether romantic or not) right now where you're aware that this is going on?

It can be overwhelming trying to navigate how best to deal with gaslighting, especially if you want to save the relationship it is taking place in.

We spoke to relationship experts and psychologists to find out the best way to safely speak to someone about their gaslighting behaviour while protecting your own mental health – and how to decide whether your relationship is actually worth saving.

Jessica Alderson, Co-Founder and Relationship Expert at So Syncd, urges anyone being gaslit not to feel like they're being unreasonable by wanting to address the situation.

She tells Metro.co.uk: 'When someone is gaslighting you, you might feel like you're going crazy, or that you're not really sure what's happening,

'You may want to break things off with someone as soon as you notice signs of gaslighting but if you do want to stay with them, there are measures you can take to increase your chances of resolving the situation.

'Talking things through with friends or family can help you gain clarity and give you confidence that you aren't misreading situations.

'Sit your partner down and explain calmly and rationally how their behaviour is affecting you, using specific examples.

'Using clear examples will help them understand what you're talking about and why their behaviour isn't acceptable.

'There's a chance that they may become defensive or try to deny what you're saying. In this case, it's best to end the relationship.

'However, if they are willing to listen to you and they genuinely want to change, you may be able to work things out, if you want to.'

The key to having a conversation with someone about gaslighting is keeping calm, says Jessica, noting that your partner's (or family member or friend's) reaction to being confronted is a big indicator of whether or not the relationship is worth salvaging.

'When having the conversation, try to avoid getting defensive or emotional and explain what you need to change in order for the relationship to continue,' she recommends.

'Make sure to actively listen to your partner. To maximise your chance of the best outcome, try to stay non-judgemental, kind, and supportive towards them.

'If they are emotionally mature and care about you, they should be sorry for their actions and how they made you feel.'

'It may take some time for your partner's behaviour to change but most importantly, you should notice consistent momentum towards reaching a healthy relationship dynamic. Your partner should show consistent willingness and be accepting of any feedback.

'For example, if you point out that they are showing signs of gaslighting again, they should apologise and immediately amend their approach.

'It's important to remember that even if you do need to occasionally point them in the right direction, not all of the change should come from you.

'They have to be willing to make significant amends – if you don't see any noticeable differences in their behaviour after having the conversation, you should end the relationship to protect your well-being.'

*Names have been changed

14 September 2022

The above information is reprinted with kind permission from *Metro* & DMG Media Licensing.
© 2024 Associated Newspapers Ltd

www.metro.co.uk

Why victims of domestic abuse don't leave – four experts explain

An article by The Conversation.

By Cassandra Wiener, Senior Lecturer in Law, City, University of London, Alison Gregory, Research Fellow, University of Bristol, Michaela Rogers, Senior Lecturer in Social Work, University of Sheffield and Sandra Walklate, Eleanor Rathbone Chair of Sociology, University of Liverpool

For anyone aware of someone – a friend, a colleague, a family member – experiencing abuse and violence at home, one of the biggest questions is often why don't they just walk away? It can be difficult to understand the extent of the coercive control and the practical hurdles in getting out, not to mention the complex feelings a survivor of abuse has to unpack. Four experts discuss why survivors might not ask for help, or feel unable to leave.

Fear and control

Cassandra Wiener, Senior Lecturer in Law, City, University of London

Coercive control is a calculated strategy of domination. A perpetrator begins by grooming their victim, thereby gaining trust and access. They then make their victim afraid – usually, but not always, by instigating the fear of physical or sexual violence. Fear is what makes threats credible. And it is when a threat is credible that a demand becomes coercive.

Research has shown that an abuser will exert control by restricting access to family and friends, money and transport, thereby isolating the victim and making it harder for them to resist. The victim experiences constant, generalised anxiety – what psychologists term a state of siege – that they have not moderated their behaviour sufficiently to avert catastrophe.

Contrary to what people often assume – that the victim chooses to stay; that they have options; that employing those options would keep them safe – research has shown that leaving is in fact dangerous. The control continues once the relationship is over but changes in emphasis from attempting to keep the victim in the relationship to trying to destroy them for leaving it.

Accommodation, childcare, support and finances

Michaela Rogers, Senior Lecturer in Social Work, University of Sheffield

For victims with children, practical and psychological barriers to ending an abusive relationship can overlap. Economic abuse often means the victim is left with low confidence and without the knowledge they need to manage their own finances and support themselves and their children. They feel guilty for removing children from their parent, their home, pets and school. They worry about moving them away from family and friends.

There may be delays in securing appropriate housing and a new school due to a shortage of social housing. There may also be a lack of affordable childcare or poor transport links. Conversely, some survivors may be tasked with daily trips back to their former neighbourhood to take children to school with the attendant risk each journey brings that they encounter their abuser.

Research shows that survivors of domestic abuse who have insecure immigration status may fear being deported. They may have little or no spoken English or access to interpreters. And they may hold concerns about managing day-to-day if they have no independent income or the right to access benefits or appropriate state funded accommodation.

For survivors who identify as LGBTQ+, meanwhile, there are myriad barriers. They might not recognise their experiences as abuse. They may fear being outed and they may worry about social services intervening, especially in terms of child protection measures.

LGBTQ+ people often also don't know of, or think they're ineligible for, mainstream domestic violence support services. Speialist services do exist but provision across the country is very modest, particularly in rural areas.

Victims with disabilities or health conditions face further practical hurdles, particularly in terms of accommodation. For some, the abuser might also be the care giver. Those with multiple and complex needs (such as mental ill health, substance use, homelessness or offending) also often struggle to access specialist support services.

Stigma and shame

Alison Gregory, Research Fellow (Traumatised and Vulnerable Populations), University of Bristol

Domestic abuse occurs in every society and culture. And yet, despite changes over the past 50 years, we are still woefully underprepared to be confronted by the idea that domestic abuse happens to people just like us.

Many survivors feel embarrassed or ashamed that they have experienced domestic abuse. They may fear that, in deciding to end an abusive relationship, their experiences will become known to others and they will risk exposing themselves to outside opinion and judgement – that they will be treated differently as a result.

Research shows survivors are concerned, in particular, about letting their parents down. Equally, ending an abusive relationship means that a survivor is confronted with their own experiences, and they may fear having to make sense of those experiences.

Love

Alison Gregory and Sandra Walklate, Chair of Sociology, University of Liverpool

Love can be an incredibly powerful reason why people remain in an abusive relationship, why they don't feel they can leave, or why they leave and then return. And it is, perhaps, one of the hardest reasons to understand. Research shows that survivors themselves become frustrated that their love, concern and care for the abuser has kept them ensnared.

A 2021 analysis of responses to the #WhyIStayed Twitter campaign reveals how complex these feelings can be. It also speaks to the powerful influence that social commentaries around relationships, marriage and the family have. Some women tweeted, 'Marriage is forever', 'I didn't wanna run when we hit a rough patch' and 'Children need a father'.

Further, the study shows the power that social expectations on romance and love exert. As one person tweeted, 'The first time he hits you, you tell yourself it was an isolated incident. He's remorseful. You forgive. Life is normal again.' Research has shown that that forgiveness stems from a victim's desire to maintain the relationship, as being a primary life goal, even at the expense of their own safety.

Abusers, conversely, can be wily and skilful when it comes to manipulating a survivor's feelings of love. They will premise coercive edicts with, 'If you loved me, you would…'. They will also use survivors' feelings of care and concern to try to prevent them from leaving, commonly making threats to harm or kill themselves if they do. Abusers know that the thought of potential harm to the abuser will cause the survivor distress and possibly feelings of guilt (even though the survivor has done nothing wrong).

Survivors may be asked by incredulous friends, relatives and professionals, 'How can you still love them after what they've done?' This sees many survivors stay silent about their residual feelings, which, in itself, is dangerous. Love is a strong motivator, and if we don't give permission for it to be voiced, we risk alienating survivors and further isolating them – which is just what abusers want.

15 February 2022

Discuss

In small groups, discuss some of the reasons that someone may choose to stay in an abusive relationship. Are there any other reasons that you can think of that aren't listed in this article?

Write

Imagine you are an agony aunt/uncle. You have received an email from a reader requesting advice on how they can safely leave an abusive relationship. What advice do you give them? Write your reply to them.

THE CONVERSATION

The above information is reprinted with kind permission from The Conversation.
© 2010-2024, The Conversation Trust (UK) Limited

Mother of teenager murdered by ex warns 'end of a relationship is the most dangerous time in a woman's life'

As knife crime against women and girls rises, Lydia Patrick talks to the families who have lost their loved ones to violent ex-partners.

A grieving mother whose 17-year-old daughter was killed by an ex-boyfriend has warned that the ending of a relationship is the most dangerous time in a woman's life.

Carole Gould has relentlessly campaigned for justice for women killed by men since her daughter Ellie was stabbed and strangled to death by her partner of three months after she ended the relationship.

Thomas Griffiths was sentenced to life imprisonment with a minimum term of 12 and a half years in 2019 after he walked into Ellie's family home, strangled her then stabbed her 13 times, attempting to frame the attack as a suicide by inserting the knife in the side of her neck.

Mrs Gould, 53, is hoping the government's consultation on knife crime will address a legal loophole and allow for tougher sentences. As it stands, murderers who kill their victims with a knife in the home face a 15-year sentencing starting point while sentences for those outside the home face at least 25.

It comes as the *Independent* reveals knife crime against women is at a five-year high after obtaining data from 26 police forces across England, Wales, and Northern Ireland through the Freedom of Information Act.

Mrs Gould is petrified her daughter's killer could harm another woman as he is set to be released before he turns 30.

'She'd only been going out with him for a few months,' her mother said. 'There were warning signs from the start, she'd only been going out with him a few days and he was saying how much he was going to spend on her for her birthday, he was clingy with her at school and possessive.'

'The weird thing was he lied to her, saying his family had two villas including one with a swimming pool in Mallorca. He was clearly a compulsive liar.

'It was her first relationship so it was exciting to her to start with and she would see him most nights after school.'

Mrs Gould says Griffiths was jealous at the prospect of Ellie moving away to university: 'Her friends disclosed to me he had become quite clingy with her in the common room and that he was talking about marriage and kids.

'The day before it happened she was in the common room playing a game and her top went up a bit and he pulled at her.

'She told him to back off and he wouldn't have liked that at all. She told me about it and I told her he sounded very possessive and asked her what she wanted to do; she told me she was going to sort it out.'

The next day, after Ellie ended the relationship over text message, Griffiths killed her in her family home.

Reflecting on the toxic relationship, Ms Gould said: 'The ending of a relationship is the most dangerous time in a woman's life.'

Nick Gazzard also lost his daughter Hollie to a violent ex-boyfriend, when she was stabbed 14 times ten years ago in the Gloucester hair salon she worked in.

The 20-year-old had tried to leave Asher Maslin after he became abusive but he bombarded her with threatening messages.,

'She was receiving constant calls to the point she was having to turn her phone off at night, constant texts, he was always appearing when she was out with friends,' her father said.

Mr Gazzard, 59, set up a trust in her memory and now educates others on the warning signs of an abusive relationship. Commenting on the rise in violence against women and girls, he said: 'She lived at home under my roof but we had no idea it was going on. Now we know the warning signs – there were constant calls, he was always appearing when she was out with friends.

'A lot of people think 'it won't happen to me' but domestic abuse is not selective, it does not matter how rich you are, what background you are from and what your parents do.'

Mr Gazzard explained his concerns about problematic male role models online which he believes has led to an increase in sexist attitudes towards women and girls.

'Some of the influencers that are around are not good role models to men; I think negative attitudes towards women have increased. We see and hear misogynistic comments much more than we used to.

'We need to improve awareness of these issues and give individuals the tools to be able to intervene safely when these things are happening, whether that's physical or verbal. We need to give more support to women.'

Mr Gazzard also blamed underfunding across the spectrum of public services including local councils, support services, the police, the NHS and charities for the escalating crisis.

He said: 'We cannot get any funding to be able to do what we need to do. If it weren't for charities like ours, we'd be in a hell of a mess; there is no support from the government and we have to raise it all ourselves; it's getting harder and harder due to austerity and the cost-of-living crisis.'

Valerie Forde and her 24-month-old daughter Jahzara were stabbed to death by her ex-partner Roland McKoy in March 2014.

Ms Forde also attempted to escape from her ex-partner and reported his abuse to the Metropolitan Police six weeks before she was killed. But the police recorded the incident as a 'threat to property' instead of a threat to life.

The mother had given her ex-partner until 31 March to leave their home; on that day she grew frightened of McKoy's behaviour and phoned her other daughter, who in turn called the police after hearing screams.

The Metropolitan police 'failed the two victims after they arrived at the property and left after six minutes,' an Independent Police Complaints Commission (IPCC) investigation concluded in June 2021.

At the time, Commander Lucy D'Orsi said: 'I have apologised to Valerie's family for our failings during the investigation into the abuse that Valerie suffered.

'I cannot begin to imagine how difficult this time has been for Valerie's family and the impact it has had and continues to have upon them.

'An independent review has also been carried out. The learning from that review will assist us in how we deal with some of the most vulnerable members of the community, those who face domestic abuse.'

Ngozi Fulani, who set up Sistah Space to advocate for black female victims of domestic abuse in the wake of the deaths, said: 'We have seen a significant rise in reporting to us of knife or sharp instrument attacks. We find perpetrators from all different backgrounds and demographics will use weapons.'

8 January 2024

The above information is reprinted with kind permission from *The Independent*.
© independent.co.uk 2024

www.independent.co.uk

I want to leave my relationship safely

Preparing to leave

However you've kept yourself safe until now, there may come a time when you feel the only option is to leave your partner.

It's never too early or too late to leave an abusive partner. Your safety matters – if you do decide to leave, it is best to plan your exit carefully.

Careful planning is important because abusers can become more violent and controlling and their actions can continue to pose a danger after you have left too – so it's a time to be especially cautious. Remember: ending the relationship will not necessarily end the abuse. Women's Aid is here for you. You are not alone.

Thinking about leaving and making the decision to go can be a long process and may even take several attempts.

Here is a checklist of things you may want to consider in your planning stage:

- Plan to leave at a time you know your partner will not be around.

- Try to take everything you will need with you, including any important documents relating to yourself and your children. Remember: you may not be able to return later.

- Try to take your children with you, otherwise it may be difficult to have them living with you in future. You may want to contact the school to them let them know what the situation is to make sure that the head and all your children's teachers know what the situation is.

- If at all possible, try to set aside a small amount of money each week, or even open a separate bank account.

Making a safety plan

A safety plan will help you protect yourself and your children. It will also help you think about how you can increase your safety both within the relationship, and if or when you decide to leave.

Only your partner can change their behaviour and end the patterns of violence and abuse they are responsible for, but there are things you can do to minimise the risk of harm to you and your children.

You might be doing some of these things already, while others might sound very obvious, but it's worth considering each point because, joined together, they can form a very helpful plan.

Plan in advance how you might respond in different situations, including in times of crisis. This includes thinking about different options available to you. Keep with you any important and emergency telephone numbers, such as the following:

- Your local domestic abuse service
- Police domestic violence unit
- GP
- Social worker
- Children's school
- Solicitor
- Freephone 24-hour National Domestic Abuse Helpline: 0808 2000 247 .

Teach your children to call 999 in an emergency and practise what they need to say (e.g. full name, address, and telephone number). You could also teach them the Silent Solution, where a caller can press 55 to tell the 999 operator that they are in an emergency and can't speak out loud. They can also contact 999 in British Sign Language (BSL) for free by visiting the website or downloading the app.

What about neighbours? Could you trust them to give you shelter in an emergency? If so, tell them what is going on and ask them to call the police if they hear sounds of a violent attack.

Rehearse your escape plan so you and your children can get away safely in an emergency.

Pack an emergency bag for you and your children and hide it somewhere safe (e.g. at a neighbour's or friend's house). Try to avoid mutual friends or family.

Keep money with you at all times if possible, including change for bus fares.

Know where the nearest phone is and if you have a mobile, try to keep it with you at all times, fully charged. If you use, Pay As You Go, make sure it's topped with credit.

Consider your safety options around tech. It's important not to do these steps before leaving, as they could result in an escalation in the abuse, but it's good to familiarise yourself with the steps. Soon after leaving, change your passwords to something the perpetrator will not be able to guess, particularly your banking and email accounts. If you want to, you can talk to your bank in confidence to let them know about your situation; they may be able to help protect your account. You can also add two-factor authentication to online banking, email, and social media accounts to add an additional layer of security. Two-factor authentication requires an additional login credential to access your account. You should turn your phone's location services off so the perpetrator cannot track you; this can be done in your phone's settings.

Know the safest place in your house and if you suspect your partner is about to attack you, try to go there (e.g. somewhere near an exit where you can access a telephone). Avoid the kitchen or garage where there are likely to be knives or other weapons; and avoid rooms where you might be trapped, such as the bathroom, or where you might be shut into a cupboard or other small space.

Be prepared to leave the house in an emergency. If you drive, keep your car keys in a safe and accessible place and make sure your car has petrol in the tank at all times.

If the abuse continues

If the harassment, threats, or abuse continue after you have left, try to keep detailed records of each incident, including the date and time it occurred, what was said or done, and – if possible – take photographs of damage to your property or injuries to yourself or others.

If a perpetrator of abuse injures you, see your GP or go to hospital for treatment and ask them to document your visit.

If you have an injunction with a power of arrest, or there is a restraining order in place, you should ask the police to enforce this; and if the perpetrator is in breach of any court order, you could also tell your solicitor if you have one.

In an emergency, always call the police on 999. Remember, if you can't speak out loud, you can press 55 so that the operator knows you need help. You can also video call 999 to communicate in BSL for free by visiting the 999 BSL website or downloading the app.

Support services near me

The Women's Aid Domestic Abuse Directory contains details of local, regional, and national services specialising in violence against women and girls including domestic abuse, sexual violence, forced marriage and stalking/harassment.

Getting medical treatment

As a result of domestic abuse, you may need medical treatment both immediately and in the long term.

If you have been injured, try to get treatment straight away if possible. You could visit your GP, go to an NHS Walk-in Centre, an Accident and Emergency department or Minor Injuries Unit at your local hospital.

Even though you may feel scared, you can tell medical staff how the injury occurred and ask them to record it. This may prove to be vital evidence in any future court proceedings: for example, if you make an application for an injunction; if there is a contact or residence dispute over your children; or if your abuser is prosecuted for a criminal offence. With your permission, health service staff and GPs can photograph injuries. When signed and dated, they can be useful additional evidence tools in court. If you think you might be pregnant, tell the doctor or nurse as you may need to be examined by a midwife to ensure that the baby has not been affected by the abuse.

This is what you should expect from a health professional. If your experience is not helpful, you may want to reach out to the manager of that service, or contact Women's Aid for some further guidance.

If you are worried about your health and don't want to go to your GP, you could ring the NHS non-emergency number on 111 (available 24 hours). NHS online provides information on health services and links to other agencies and self-help organisations.

Sexual abuse

If you have experienced sexual abuse, try to get yourself to a place where you feel safe. See if a friend or someone you trust can be with you and talk to them about what has happened.

If you need urgent medical care or attention, call 999, ask for an ambulance or go straight to your nearest Accident and Emergency department.

If a sexual assault has just taken place and you feel able to report the incident to the police or attend a sexual assault referral centre (SARC), you may want to preserve as much evidence as possible. Try not to wash or wash your clothes in order to preserve forensic evidence.

SARCs offer a range of support services, including crisis care, examinations, emergency contraception, and sexually transmitted infection (STI) testing. A SARC examination can check for injuries, infections and collect possible evidence. If you decide you want to report an assault to the police, they can arrange for you to speak with a trained officer who can support you with the next steps. You can find your local SARC here.

If you don't feel able to talk to a friend or family member, you can contact your nearest Rape Crisis organisation or call their free helpline on 0808 802 9999, open 24/7 or use their webchat service.

What will happen when I leave?

What is a refuge?

A refuge is a safe house where women and children who have experienced domestic abuse can live free from fear. The address, and sometimes even the phone numbers, must be kept confidential to ensure the safety of all its residents.

Who can go into a refuge?

Any woman who needs to escape from domestic abuse can go into a refuge. It does not matter whether you are married to the absuer, living with the abuser, or whether you have children or not. There are also refuges specifically run by and for Black and minoritised women.

There are refuges throughout the UK, and depending on space and availability, you can choose where you would like to go. Refuges may be unlikely to accept women from their immediate local area for safety reasons. This will depend on the individual refuge and their safety policies.

Women's Aid's No Woman Turned Away (NWTA) Project provides dedicated support to women who face barriers in accessing a refuge space. A team of specialist domestic abuse practitioners receive referrals and work with survivors of domestic abuse, advocating for them when needed, to find safe accommodation. Barriers could include (but are not limited to) having mental health support needs, disabilities, or having a larger family, for example.

Engaging with the NWTA Project does not always guarantee a refuge space and there can sometimes be limitations to the support provided. If you are needing any further information regarding the NWTA Project, you can ask a support worker via our Live Chat service.

Life in a refuge

You may be placed in a big refuge with space for many women and children; however, others are much smaller.

Your children are welcome to come with you to refuge. Most refuges with be able to offer you your own room to share with your children, and some will have self-contained family units.

Many refuges have disabled access, and staff and volunteers who can support you or your children if you have additional needs.

In the refuge, there may be communal spaces like a living room, TV room, kitchen, and playroom which will be shared with other refuge residents. In some refuges, the bathroom may be communal too.

You'll cook for yourself and your children. You and the other residents can cook together at meal times or decide whether you take turns and eat separately. You can socialise as much or as little as you choose.

Refuges have their own codes of conduct for the day-to-day running of the house. These usually cover things like bedtimes for children, incoming calls, and rotas for using the washing machine.

Remember, you'll be asked to sign a licence agreement covering the terms under which you can stay in the refuge. This will include the rent, how long you can stay, and any guidelines to keep you safe. These may include rules on the use of alcohol and drugs, confidentiality, and who can visit.

Can I bring my teenage sons with me?

It depends. Some refuges allow boys up to the age of 16, while others cannot take boys over the age of 13 or 14. Very few refuges will accept male children over the age of 16. Talk to a support worker on Live Chat for additional support you could access around this.

How do I arrange refuge accommodation?

A Women's Aid support worker can search for current vacancies via the Live Chat service. You also can call the freephone 24-hour National Domestic Violence Helpline (run by the charity Refuge) on 0808 2000 247. The helpline is also available in BSL from Monday to Friday between 10am and 6pm.

Many refuge organisations also have public contact numbers which you can contact yourself. Visit the Women's Aid Directory to find your local domestic abuse services.

Social services, the police, or the housing department will also be able to help you find a refuge.

When you are ready to start looking for a refuge, you can contact the Live Chat or the National Domestic Abuse Helpline. Sometimes you can go into refuge on the same day; however, the process could also take some time. Support workers can discuss with you where in the country you may like to go; however, please be aware refuges can be limited on a particular day, so you might want to consider being flexible around location.

If you would like Women's Aid to search for current vacancies with you via Live Chat, the following information will be needed:

- Some background information including details of the domestic abuse
- Ages of any children who may be going with you
- Information on any support needs you and your children may have.

A support worker can look for any suitable refuge spaces. If there are any suitable spaces, they can give you their contact details and any further information you may need to know about the refuge. You will then be encouraged to directly contact the refuge, so they can go through their own referral process with you. If you are unable to do these steps, perhaps due to financial or language barriers, a Women's Aid support worker can call the refuge on your behalf.

Once you have been accepted into a refuge, they will provide you with more details and discuss with you how to get there. They will also give you more information on safety at the refuge. If they give you the address and the location of the refuge, it is very important that you keep this information to yourself. Take care not to leave any of the information behind because it will leave you at risk of being traced.

The above information is reprinted with kind permission from Women's Aid.
© 2024 Women's Aid

www.womensaid.org.uk

Chapter 3

Preventing and Surviving Abuse

Domestic abuse victims to be given up to £2,500 to help them flee partners

'Kids, lack of money and confidence, and fear of reprisal keep so many victims locked into dangerous and harmful situations for far too long,' says Minister for Victims and Safeguarding.

By Maya Oppenheim, Women's Correspondent

Domestic abuse victims will be given up to £2,500 to help them escape their situation under a new government scheme.

The Home Office has announced a £2 million pot for people who lack the money to escape an abusive partner.

Victims can claim a payment of up to £500 for staples such as food and nappies, or can apply for up to £2,500 to go towards housing costs. The payments will be available from 31 January 2024.

The fund builds on a pilot scheme funded by the Home Office and delivered in conjunction with Women's Aid last year, which helped more than 600 people get to safety.

The Minister for Victims and Safeguarding, Laura Farris, said: 'Women leave abusive partners at what is often the lowest point in their lives. The most common issues – kids, lack of money and confidence, fear of reprisal – keep so many victims locked into dangerous and harmful situations for far too long.

'I am proud this fund has helped over 600 people to escape their abusers and find safety, and hope this additional £2m will help hundreds more find peace and rebuild their lives.'

Previous research reported by *The Independent* found that nearly three-quarters of domestic abuse victims said the spiralling cost-of-living crisis had stopped them from escaping their abusive partner or made it trickier for them to flee.

The domestic abuse commissioner for England and Wales, Nicole Jacobs, said: 'It will be a lifeline for many, helping victims to flee abuse and rebuild their lives.

'I hope to see this critical funding reach as many victims and survivors as possible, including those who face the most significant barriers to support.'

The scheme, which will continue until March 2025, will be rolled out through a network of local frontline services in England and Wales.

Farah Nazeer, Chief Executive of Women's Aid, said: 'Domestic abuse affects a huge number of people, many of whom face additional challenges when it comes to receiving the life-changing support that they need.'

Ms Nazeer said that more than three-quarters of applicants during last year's pilot of the fund used their money to replace or buy essential items, having escaped their abuser with no money.

'By allowing more survivors to escape their abusers, we are taking steps in the right direction to building a society in which domestic abuse is no longer tolerated,' she said.

For help or support contact the National Domestic Abuse Helpline, which is open 24/7 365 days per year on 0808 2000 247, or go to its website at www.nationaldahelpline.org.uk

9 January 2024

The above information is reprinted with kind permission from *The Independent*.
© independent.co.uk 2024

www.independent.co.uk

Tina Turner: the singer's resilience and defiance were typical of a survivor of intimate partner abuse

An article from The Conversation.

By Dr Sarah Tatton, PhD Candidate and Associate Lecturer in Criminology, Sheffield Hallam University

There was something elemental about the ferocity of Tina Turner's stage strut and the grit in her voice. Her death last week, aged 83, was met with an outpouring of tributes celebrating her musical prowess. But as we mourn her passing, it's worth noting that Tina was also a model survivor of intimate partner violence.

In 1981, following her split from husband Ike Turner, Tina Turner began to speak openly about the years of abuse she had endured during their marriage. No charges related to domestic abuse were ever brought, and Ike Turner denied the accusations. Yet, over the decades Turner told a story familiar and inspiring to many other survivors.

Turner is rightly held up as a trailblazer for speaking publicly about her experience of intimate partner violence. But media coverage of Ike and Tina's relationship has often solely focused on Ike's physical violence.

Physical violence sells newspapers. It's easy for observers to understand and widely considered the worst form of abuse by those who have never experienced it. When Turner first spoke publicly about her experience in the early 1980s, 'domestic violence' was thought of as episodic physical assault, perhaps triggered by stress or even by the victim themselves.

However, Turner's accounts of her relationship revealed a pattern of coercive control. This understanding of abuse is something the world is still trying to catch up with.

Not only was Ike physically and sexually violent, but he ensnared Turner in a web of other controlling tactics, including financial control, emotional manipulation, control of her identity and a pattern of charm and 'love-bombing'.

It is this web of domination over victims that disempowers them and often prevents them from leaving a violent relationship. Many survivors report the emotional and psychological strategies of abuse as the longest lasting and most damaging elements of an abusive relationship. For experts in the field of intimate partner violence, Ike's behaviour is textbook coercive control.

What makes Turner's escape inspiring is the many layers of threat she faced and resisted beyond physical violence.

A strong (and vulnerable) black woman

Much of the media coverage of Turner's victim-survivor status overlooks the fact that as a black woman she walked a fine line in speaking publicly about her experiences.

Research has repeatedly found that intersectional issues are faced by black women who speak out and seek support for abuse. Intersectionality describes multiple challenges or disadvantages faced by an individual with overlapping social identities, such as being a black woman. Stereotypes are one example.

In criminological theory, the stereotypical 'ideal victim' is perceived as weak and submissive. This stereotype has been attached to the notion of the 'battered woman' even though it does not match most survivor experiences of resistance.

There remains a widespread lack of understanding of abuse survivors as resourceful and resilient – as opposed to weak. The stereotype of the 'strong black woman', who is fiercely loving, feisty and independent is even more at odds with the 'battered woman' trope. Many black female survivors are criminalised as a result of this dissonance.

The black male identity is likewise affected by deeply embedded stereotypes. Most survivors, including Turner, offer loyalty as a reason for keeping abuse private, fearing social repercussions if their partner is labelled as an abuser.

Speaking out publicly as a black woman was complex for Turner, and as other black women have expressed, her bravery and steadfastness has inspired many others to follow suit.

More than a survivor

As media coverage over recent days has pointed out, Turner refused to be defined by her experiences. In this regard, she is typical of a survivor of abuse, not an exception.

Stereotypes of abuse victims as weak and submissive often lead to popular coverage which assumes that victimhood dominates a survivor's social identity. In my research, however, survivors often tell me that they 'refused to be a victim'. What they mean as they discuss their circumstances is that they are so much more than the stereotypical 'victim' of domestic abuse.

Turner was the epitome of the victim-survivor, breaking free and living her life to the full. Not all victims are privileged to have the resources to live a rockstar lifestyle. On the contrary, many are left financially destitute and often have their reputation dismantled, but all are far more than 'victims'. Domestic abuse victims to be given up to £2,500 to help them flee partners

'Kids, lack of money and confidence, and fear of reprisal keep so many victims locked into dangerous and harmful situations for far too long,' says minister for victims and safeguarding

In the month before she died, Turner was asked how she wanted to be remembered. For all the inspiration and the enormous influence she had as a survivor of intimate partner abuse, she wanted to be remembered for the person she was and the work she did – as the queen of rock and roll.

31 May 2023

Brainstorm

In small groups, think of some stereotypes about victims of domestic abuse.

Write

In pairs, write a list of things that can be classed as coercive control.

Read

Find two recent news stories about celebrities who have been victims and survivors of domestic abuse. Compare and contrast the articles.

Are there any differences in the way the victim/survivor is written about due to age, race or gender?

Is the writer sympathetic to the victim/survivor, or are they victim-blaming?

Write some notes on your findings.

THE CONVERSATION

The above information is reprinted with kind permission from The Conversation.
© 2010-2024, The Conversation Trust (UK) Limited

www.theconversation.com

'When you admit the truth, you have to take action': the phoneline helping abusers change their behaviour

The number of abusers calling a helpline over their actions has surged. But are they really willing to change? Maya Oppenheim listens in to find out.

Paul* manages his finances 'to the penny.' If he buys a packet of crisps when he is out, he records it in his account book at home, noting down the exact amount. But it's not just his own spending he keeps a watchful eye over. If Paul's wife Susie* buys anything when she's out, Paul knows – and he records that too.

In fact, Paul keeps tabs on quite a few parts of Susie's life. He and his wife share all their emails and texts with each other. They do 'everything together,' he says.

Paul is going through the details of his marriage after calling an anonymous and confidential helpline, run by the charity Respect, set up for people who have been violent or abusive to their partners or families – or fear they could be. Paul's children have accused him of perpetrating a concerted campaign of domestic abuse against his wife.

Although he claims he is desperately trying to work out whether he abuses, controls or coerces his wife, he also appears unable to look at his own behaviour clearly and honestly.

'We share everything, we make joint decisions,' he tells a helpline worker. 'It is a loving, caring relationship. We are very fortunate our chemistry is the same as when we were courting. We do silly things teenagers do. There is no oppression. Everything we do is healthy and happy.'

I am privy to all of this because I am listening in on the calls – with the callers' permission – to find out more about how the helpline tries to help those who carry out domestic abuse.

Paul is one of a growing number of callers seeking support from Respect. Exclusive data from the charity, shared with *The Independent*, reveals the number of people ringing their helpline has surged by 28 per cent from 2018/2019 to 2022/2023 – rising from 5,521 calls to 7,093 calls.

Another call I listen to involves a man saying his former partner was claiming he had threatened to kill her and was abusive – but he denied this. Other phone calls feature men looking for perpetrator programmes to help them tackle their domestic abuse.

One woman in her mid-twenties also rings the helpline to admit she has been emotionally and physically abusive to her male partner. She says she has had fantasies of treating her partner even more badly. The caller explains she has acted similarly with ex-partners and has been this way since she started dating people aged 18.

But it's clear most domestic abusers do not seek help. While police in England and Wales receive an average of over 100 calls an hour on domestic abuse across a year – and between two and three women are killed by a current or

> 'We want to understand what triggered the call and it is actually, and sadly, very rare that someone will call the helpline completely out of the blue. There is usually some incident that triggered it.'
> – Ippo Panteloudakis

male ex-partner every week in England and Wales – calls to the helpline are few and far between.

The rise in calls during the COVID-19 pandemic is likely to have been linked to an increase in domestic abuse, as lockdown measures exacerbated pre-existing patterns of behaviour. But it is less clear what is causing the continued surge.

Ippo Panteloudakis, Head of Services at Respect, says there was an increased awareness of domestic abuse during the pandemic, with the helpline now more promoted on social media.

But Mr Panteloudakis, who has listened to thousands of calls which come into the helpline, also attributes the rise in calls to a greater emphasis on perpetrators changing their behaviour in wider society. Other factors involve asking for help becoming more socially acceptable – but also the cost-of-living crisis exacerbating abusive behaviour.

'Where it already exists, it's a situation that makes things much worse,' he adds. 'It's more of an opportunity to have conflict in the relationship and where someone perpetrates abuse, that can be just another reason for them to be unhappy and want to be controlling and use violence and abuse.'

Mr Panteloudakis, who has been working at Respect for almost two decades, says their first port of call when someone rings the helpline is to try to understand why the person is calling.

'That is not as obvious as it may sound,' he adds. 'We want to understand what triggered the call and it is actually, and sadly, very rare that someone will call the helpline completely out of the blue. There is usually some incident that triggered it. It could be that they were violent or abusive very recently and there was police involvement. Or maybe the wider family found out that they are perpetrating domestic abuse.'

Another example he gives involves their partner choosing to leave them – sometimes with the children in tow. Mr Panteloudakis says all of these scenarios can invoke a desire in someone to change. 'It may not be a sustained feeling that you see through, but at least there is a window of opportunity, and that is what we're trying to keep open,' he adds.

Helpline workers seek to differentiate between the person and their behaviour, Mr Panteloudakis explains. 'We're not trying to label someone as a monster or anything like that,' he adds. 'And that is a constant fear that perpetrators have – that they will be judged. But we identify behaviours that are harmful. We explain how they are harmful to others – to the survivor and the children, to increase their empathy as a way to motivate them to access help.'

But Mr Panteloudakis says this does not stop perpetrators from being 'manipulative' and 'minimising' their violence and abuse, adding they seek to root out disingenuous callers who are only ringing to keep their partners happy. He also reflects on the fact most perpetrators of domestic abuse are not able to 'connect dots' and see patterns in their behaviour.

'But for others, on some level, there is some defence mechanism because if you connect those dots, you start seeing who you really are,' he adds. 'And that is something that perpetrators don't want to do. Because when you start to understand who you really are, that you are not this nice, charming guy, but someone who on occasion or frequently uses violence and abuse towards their partner. When you admit the truth to yourself, then the next step is you have to do something about it.'

Mr Panteloudakis states they have a range of safety mechanisms in place – such as not speaking to anyone if they gauge they are not alone, and ensuring callers do not hang up feeling angry.

'They might become angry on the phone and that has to be managed very, very skillfully and respectfully,' he adds. 'The training for helpline workers is all bespoke.'

On the rise in callers, Charlotte Kneer, Chief Executive of Reigate and Banstead Women's Aid refuges in Surrey, says it could signal 'the beginnings of a culture shift' of perpetrators being more eager to address their behaviour due to domestic abuse becoming more 'societally unacceptable'.

'People seemed in the pandemic to take an interest in domestic abuse because it was so much more talked about,' Ms Kneer, a domestic abuse survivor whose violent partner was jailed for seven years in 2011, adds. 'Potentially perpetrators could have become more aware of their behaviour.'

Another theory Ms Kneer posits is tied to the increase in money the Domestic Abuse Act has provided to services. She questions whether the funding has led to more victims accessing services across the country, which is in turn sparking more abusers to seek support.

'The most likely point the perpetrator is going to access a perpetrator service is when the victim is going to leave and end the relationship,' she adds. 'I suspect often perpetrators are accessing the service not because they recognise their behaviour is abominable but to prove to their victim they are trying to seek help and hold onto that relationship. It is great perpetrators are reaching out but it doesn't mean they have great insight into their behaviour.'

*Paul and Susie's names have been changed to protect their identities

27 October 2023

The above information is reprinted with kind permission from *The Independent*.
© independent.co.uk 2024

www.independent.co.uk

'The law is cold. It doesn't reflect the life lost': mothers of murdered women tell their stories

Grieving parents of two young women killed by their ex-boyfriends launch a new film to step up their campaign for justice.

By Alice Fisher

A new campaign film keeps the pressure on the Ministry of Justice to change the minimum sentence for domestic murder. *The Changes That We Can Make* features Carole Gould and Julie Devey, two mothers who have been campaigning since February 2020 on behalf of their daughters, Ellie and Poppy.

Sixth-form student Ellie Gould, 17, was murdered by her ex-boyfriend, Thomas Griffiths, on 3 May 2019. Quantitative trading analyst Poppy Devey Waterhouse, 24, was murdered by her ex-boyfriend, Joe Atkinson, on 14 December 2018. Though these were frenzied attacks involving multiple injuries, and the killers tried to hide their crimes, the guidelines for murder sentencing meant that both received minimum tariffs set at less than 20 years in prison. Atkinson's was fixed at 16 years; Griffiths got 12 and a half years.

Gould and Devey's documentary was directed by Levi James, a final-year film student at the University of the West of England, who knew Poppy from college. It highlights the way the circumstances of a killing can deeply affect the time served – and shows how domestic murderers often avoid long sentences.

Their campaign aim was two-fold: to change youth and adult sentencing in domestic homicides. Griffiths was sentenced to 12 and a half years for murdering Ellie because he was five months away from his 18th birthday when he committed the crime. The law viewed him simply as a juvenile: even though he was 17, his sentence was the same as would have been given to a 10-year-old.

Thanks to Gould and Devey's work, a sliding scale for juvenile sentencing was introduced in March this year. Under the new rules, teenage killers could now serve up to 27 years for terrorist attacks. A 17 year old's sentence for domestic homicide would be increased from 12 years to 14 years. This will be known as Ellie's Law.

The two women are continuing their fight to have the sentencing rules on the murder weapon and the location of the killing changed.

Currently, if the crime occurs in the home, the killer automatically faces a lesser sentence. The same murder committed in the street receives 10 years' more prison time. If the domestic murderer uses a weapon found at the scene rather than bringing one with him, the tariff is 15 years, as the crime is seen as without premeditation. A murderer who brings the weapon will receive 25 years. Both Atkinson and Griffiths used knives found at the scene, which instantly reduced their maximum possible sentence by 10 years.

Gould and Devey want domestic murder tariffs to reflect the severity of the crime rather than the location of the killing. The new law would be known as Poppy's Law.

The Justice Secretary, Robert Buckland, has watched *The Changes That We Can Make* and promised to meet with Gould and Devey to update them on the sentencing review currently under way. 'We've received an email saying Buckland was deeply moved by the film,' says Gould. 'He wants to set up a meeting to discuss the review – though he says Poppy's Law can't be added to the police crime sentencing and courts bill, which is disappointing.'

The pair want the film to be seen by the general public to raise awareness of their campaign and the laws surrounding domestic homicide.

'I want people who see this film to be aware of the emotional, mental and physical impact on our lives,' says Devey. 'I also want them to be alert to the sentences domestic murderers receive and to what these perpetrators did. There's just no way that a normal-thinking person could see these killers as less dangerous because of where these murders took place.'

Gould asks anyone who would like to help the campaign to contact their MP. 'Before Griffiths was sentenced, a barrister told us what sentence he would get. He said the law is cold, it doesn't reflect the life that's lost. You just want to scream – it should reflect the life that's lost. It should reflect the damage to the victim's family. What sort of justice system have we got that doesn't take any of those things into account?'

24 July 2021

Watch

Watch the short documentary *The Changes That We Can Make* (available on YouTube).

https://youtu.be/EhBEbMQblG8?si=rdw3hFXRAt-f473U

The above information is reprinted with kind permission from *The Guardian*.
© 2024 Guardian News and Media Limited

www.theguardian.com

Asha's story

At first, I was in denial and didn't want to think about the fact I was being abused – but people were looking out for me all along and never gave up on me.

For instance, my previous employer really cared about me and kept reaching out even though I kept making excuses for the abuse. At the time, I wasn't in the right state of mind to fully accept the help or acknowledge what was happening to me. I was pushing away reality as a way of coping and defending myself against the pain and trauma.

Then one day someone left me alone in an office with the contact details for Women's Aid and encouraged me to get in touch. It was a relief to finally start accessing support but also very painful because I was in the process of finally acknowledging that I was being abused. I felt a huge sense of shame and guilt.

I was at the start of a long journey, beginning to acknowledge that I was being treated badly in my relationship. For the first time, I began to think about the word 'abuse' internally, but could still not say it out loud.

During that period, I left my relationship for a second time but soon went back. There was nothing anyone could do at the time to get me out – but I still felt their support and valued it deeply.

One friend tried to call out my ex on some of his behaviour, but he didn't even need to react because I was soon jumping to his defence while he just deflected it all back on her, saying she was bad news. But still she supported me, gently encouraging me to focus on how I felt about myself irrespective of the relationship. That was the start of coming back to myself and gaining consciousness. It was massive.

My ex always found ways of isolating me so my friend and I didn't have much time together but when she did get me alone, she would simply ask: 'How are you feeling? How are you treating yourself?'.

She had an anti-anxiety book and we did one of the exercises together which involved her writing down some of my favourite experiences of the year and helping me to vocalise what they meant; spelling out to me the positives that were evidenced by these experiences. I carried that note around with me for a long time. My friend still feels she did not do enough to help me but this alone was so fundamentally important.

The truth is I was just not ready to leave for a long time. It takes so much to leave and it took a long time after my first contact with Women's Aid and a year after writing that note with my friend that I finally broke free.

In the end my body took over and decided for me. I became ill and couldn't work due to surgery. I was trying to recover at home and the truth suddenly came to me as a simple, unemotional fact: 'If nothing about my situation changes, my body will give up and I will die.' I could feel myself slipping away. My body had helped me to survive for a long time but now it was just not bothering to keep going.

It was a purely physical feeling, there was no rational thinking or emotion involved. My body was trying to escape, to leave the situation by blacking out or just sleeping. At the same time it was telling me something much more loudly than in the past because I had not been listening. My brain was numb, so my body was trying to talk to me instead.

I had been forced to turn off my feelings for so long because if you allow yourself to feel too much sadness or desperation, you can't survive. And so with the wisdom of my body and the support of my friends on my side, I left during the pandemic, having only just recovered from coronavirus and my surgery.

Leaving for good was the hardest thing I have ever done. However, I knew as I walked out the door that this time it was finally over.

Now that I am free from abuse there are sometimes difficult feelings which overwhelm me because I am finally in a safe place to acknowledge them. It's hard to cope when that happens but with the right support I can now work through those emotions and finally let them go. And as I go through this process, those moments occur less and less.

The journey to acknowledging abuse is a long and personal one (and there will be many setbacks) but hopefully stories like mine will help other women to realise that – with one step at a time – it is possible to reach a place of peace and safety.

The above information is reprinted with kind permission from Women's Aid.
© 2024 Women's Aid

www.womensaid.org.uk

What is Clare's Law?

The Domestic Violence Disclosure Scheme (DVDS), also known as 'Clare's Law', enables the police to disclose information to a victim or potential victim of domestic abuse. This can be information about their partner's or ex-partner's previous abusive or violent offending.

Who is Clare?

Clare Wood was murdered by her abusive ex-boyfriend in 2009 who has a history of being violent towards his partners. An inquest into Clare's murder revealed a loophole in the Data Protection Act. The loophole prevents police from sharing information about individuals with a history of violence or abuse.

Clare's father, Michael, believes this knowledge could have saved Clare's life. Michael began a passionate campaign with a vision to create a police disclosure scheme. A scheme that would allow everyone the right to know of a partner's history of violence.

Clare's Law has already saved hundreds of lives.

The 'Right to Ask' and the 'Right to Know'

The scheme has two elements:

1. The 'Right to Ask' allows friends or families to ask for more information. You can ask the police to check if your partner has a violent past. A friend or family member can also do this. If records show that an individual may be at risk, the police will consider disclosing the information.

2. The 'Right to Know' enables the police to make a disclosure if they receive concerning information. This is if the information may impact on the safety of that person's current or ex partner. This could be information arising from a criminal investigation, as well as through statutory or third-sector agency involvement, or from another source of police intelligence.

How to access Clare's Law

Contact your local police. It is as simple as going to the police station and saying 'I want to make an application under Clare's Law'.

The police will ask for two forms of ID and complete an initial risk assessment. The purpose of these initial checks is to establish if there are any immediate concerns. The police will then contact you if there is anything to disclose.

Alternately, contact a local domestic abuse support service who can support you through the process.

What to do following a disclosure

Once receiving the disclosure, a potential victim can then make informed choices about the relationships. All disclosure of the scheme requires a robust safety plan, tailored to the needs of the individual.

Statistics

- In the year ending March 2020, 8,591 individuals applied for the 'Right to Know' in England and Wales. 4,479 (52%) applications resulted in disclosure.

- In the year ending March 2020, 11,556 individuals applied for the 'Right to Ask' in England and Wales. 4,236 (37%) applications resulted in disclosure.

- Only when there is something concerning to disclose will further information be given. Bot sets of data come from the Domestic Abuse Disclosure Scheme.

Where else can I get help?

Contact the freephone 24-hour National Domestic Abuse Helpline: 0808 2000 247

Contact the ManKind Initiative for male domestic abuse victims: 01823 334244

18 October 2023

The above information is reprinted with kind permission from Maria Fogg Family Law.
© 2024 Maria Fogg Family Law Limited.

www.mariafoggfamilylaw.co.uk

Is Clare's Law working?

Dr Nicole Renehan from Durham University's Department of Sociology, together with project partners Professor Sandra Walklate (Liverpool University) and Dr Charlotte Barlow (University of Central Lancashire) discuss whether Clare's Law, otherwise known as the Domestic Violence Disclosure Scheme, is working and if it is fit for purpose.

Media coverage of Wiltshire Police's response under Clare's Law and the inquest into the domestic murder of Terri Harris, alongside her two children and their friend, has put Clare's Law back under the spotlight. Clare's Law (more formally known as the Domestic Violence Disclosure Scheme) allows the police to disclose the criminal records of those who may pose a risk to intimate partners. However, despite Home Office assurances that Clare's Law 'does work,' Terri's mother claims the scheme is 'not fit for purpose.'

Clare's Law was introduced following a highly public campaign led by Clare Wood's father who was of the view that, if only he and Clare had known more about the perpetrator's background of violence towards women then her murder would have been prevented. Yet as the Independent Police Complaints Commission (IPCC) report on Clare Wood's death evidenced, Clare was already aware of his violence towards her.

The assumption that knowledge leads to women leaving relationships is a commonly held sentiment, fundamentally misunderstanding the position many women living with domestic abuse find themselves in. Nevertheless, this scheme introduced by Teresa May's government in 2014, was heralded as an important criminal justice asset for preventing and protecting women from domestic abuse. Indeed, under the 2021 Domestic Abuse Act (England and Wales), Clare's Law was put on a statutory footing with revised guidance issued to all police forces.

Ten years on from its introduction, problems remain in delivering the intended aims of Clare's Law. It assumes it can deliver protection, yet our research funded by the British Academy suggests that such an assumption is problematic. A major problem for delivering protection is information sharing.

As our study suggests, Clare's law places too much responsibility on the victim-survivor to act on the information received (assuming it is accurate) and simultaneously reduces the responsibility of state professionals should the woman fail to act on the information given. The result is victim-blaming. Indeed, the women in our study blamed themselves and were blamed by others for the nature of their relationships. The question remains then, where and how might Clare's Law fit for women living with, or suspect they are in a relationship with, a domestic abuse perpetrator?

For the women in our study, there were three ways in which having Clare's Law information might work: when it was shared, who shared it, and how it fitted with their real lives.

The question of when information is shared is an important one. Women will only act on what they know or what they are told when they are ready to do so. The barriers to doing otherwise are both immense and well-documented in the literature. Enabling women to act includes having information but also includes having support from family, friends, having the financial resources, alternative housing opportunities and so on. Simply telling a woman, especially if she has not requested the information herself, her partner has a history of abuse is only going to add to her concerns. In the longer term, such information may assist her if the right kind of contact with the right support services are in place.

The question of who shares the information raises a slightly different issue. Clare's Law assumes information flows from criminal justice professionals (and others) to women, that they are legally prohibited from sharing outside of the disclosure process itself. The women in our study, however, reported sharing and receiving personal domestic abuse experiences from their partners' ex-partners, frequently from women previously not known to them. This is sideways or a more democratic information sharing process. The 'top-down' approach of policy seems to operate as if the democratic practices of people's real lives do not exist and/or is not meaningful for those participating in Clare's Law. Notably, women's sharing of their domestic abuse experiences, as our data illustrates, did in some cases function as a red flag prompting victim-survivors to seek a formal disclosure from the police. For others, abusive men circumvented such effort by using victim-blaming strategies to prevent them from leaving the relationship. The woman's decision to leave was a culmination of many pieces of information from various sources, suggesting agencies tasked with sharing disclosures should engage victim-survivors in ongoing conversations to explore the diverse options they might have and when they might be best placed to take them.

Our research speaks strongly to the need for policies of all kinds in relation to domestic abuse to make a space for appreciating women's real lives, especially. Women living with violence engage in safety work on a routine, daily basis, as do all women. The women who participated in our study knew how to keep themselves and their children safe. Offering them more information in the absence of any other kind of support only served to make them further responsible for the men's violence in their lives.

Adding these research findings to the catalogue of inept information sharing documented in the HM Inspectorate of Probation Report on Damien Bendall, and the recent review of Clare's Law in Wiltshire as set out by the Independent Office for Police Conduct (IOPC), the picture is clear. This scheme is not working for the women for whom it is intended either in its own terms or in theirs.

28 November 2023

The above information is reprinted with kind permission from Durham University.
© 2024 Durham University

www.durham.ac.uk

Sally's Law

People that kill a partner after years of domestic abuse and violence will now be treated more leniently under new reforms – named Sally's Law, following the case of Sally Challen.

I can't remember the exact year but we were living in the flat so it must have been around 1987. I can't remember the exact time but I know it was in the middle of the night. What I do remember, very clearly, is holding a pillow over my sleeping husband's head. I held it there for what seemed like forever. He started spluttering and I sort of 'came to' and realised what I was doing. It kind of felt like a dream but it wasn't. I think the night before, he had hit me but it really doesn't matter if he did or didn't. Perhaps he had called me a fat ****. Probably, as he called me that and other things most days. He was a very heavy sleeper – more so when he had had a drink, but again, I can't remember if he had had a drink or not. I could so easily have killed him that night and to this day, he knows nothing about it!

What would have happened to me if I had held that pillow there for just a bit longer? Well, I would have gone to prison for life probably. The things that I would have missed or that would never have happened run through my mind. I would never have had my youngest daughter or the grandchild she is carrying now. I would not have seen my eldest daughter grow up and I wouldn't have seen or probably know my granddaughter and grandson, who are my world. I would never have met my late husband, Clive. So many things. How long would I have served by now? 36 years!! Maybe someone like Justice for Women would have campaigned to get me out. Maybe not. But one thing I do know for certain is that the domestic abuse I experienced at his hands would not have been seen as important at the trial that would have almost certainly convicted me of murder.

Does this shock you? That I could so easily have committed murder? Would you have cared if you knew back then? No, I don't think so. In fact, I would have been just another woman who killed her husband and got life for doing it. End of!! There are so many women in prison *now* that this has happened to.

My point is, I know how easy it is to almost kill someone. I could so easily have held that pillow there, over his face for a few seconds, a couple of minutes longer. I didn't want him to die though. No. He was the father of my child. He was my husband. I had loved him. I simply wanted the abuse and violence to stop! Does what I nearly did that night make me a bad person? Does it make me evil? I don't think so. But I probably felt I was back then.

I imagine Sally Challen felt similar feelings. Sally Challen was sentenced to a minimum of 22 years in prison in 2011. In August, 2010, she had killed her husband of 31 years after having experienced domestic abuse, coercive control and rape for many, many years beforehand. Soon after Sally's conviction, her two son's, James and David, approached Justice for Women and asked them for help. They found Sally a new legal team and new grounds for appeal citing the domestic abuse and coercive control she had experienced in the intervening years. Four years later in 2015, coercive and controlling behaviour was made a criminal offence and this was the breakthrough Justice for Women and Sally's son's needed. At last, Sally had the grounds for appeal. In June 2019, Sally became the first woman to ever have a murder conviction quashed under the new coercive and controlling behaviour law. Sally had her sentence reduced to 14 years for manslaughter and as a result of already serving 9 years in prison, she was released. I don't know Sally but I know her son, David through my work with National Centre for Domestic Violence (NCDV). David is an official supporter of NCDV.

So why am I telling you this?

Because it has very recently been announced that people who kill a partner after enduring years of domestic abuse and/or violence will be treated more leniently by the criminal justice system. This new law will be called 'Sally's

Law'. Judges will be required to treat years of physical abuse or coercive control as a mitigating factor following the case of Sally Challen.

These changes in the law come after an independent review on domestic homicide sentencing by Clare Wade, KC, who was Sally Challen's defence barrister. This report was published in March 2023. For the first time, coercive control will be acknowledged as a mitigating circumstance for victims and survivors of domestic abuse who kill their abuser. Judges will now have to consider the sometimes years of abuse and trauma experienced by the accused, which will in turn give them a chance of a fairer trial and more sympathetic, reduced sentence.

At NCDV, which is my 'day job', I work on a Prison Partnership. In total, I am working in partnership with seven women's prisons in England. Historically, it has always been very difficult for women in prison to secure protection orders such as non-molestation orders as the courts will deem these women not at risk because they are in prison. However, there are mitigating circumstances here too. These women may not have 'officially' separated from their abuser. They haven't left the relationship. They have been put in a position where they have been temporarily removed from the abusive relationship and often are met at the gate on their release, by their abuser. NCDV helps and supports these women to secure protective orders before they are released from prison so that they do not fall straight back into the cycle of abuse.

Almost two-thirds of women in prison in the UK are reported to have experienced domestic abuse. Many are in prison for crimes associated with that domestic abuse. This can range from shoplifting or drug dealing, to assault and domestic homicide. I have spoken to women in prison who have told me that they were not listened to about the abuse they experienced which contributed to their crimes, that the abuse they experienced was not mentioned in court and how they received unfair, and harsh sentences whereas their abuser went completely unpunished even when reported. How can this be fair?

The independent review by Clare Wade, KC, highlighted that greater protection should be given to people who kill their abusers. This overhaul will also increase penalties for abusers, partners, and ex-partners who kill after a relationship has come to an end. But will this be enough? What needs to happen to prevent situations getting to this point in the first place?

It is a question that Sally Challen has given a lot of thought to. In a recent interview Sally did for *The Sun* newspaper, Sally said: 'Educating in school is good. Getting abused victims to talk to schoolchildren is good. This is learned behaviour, and often picked up from an abusive dad. 'Kids need to learn that is not normal behaviour, and this is not how you treat women.'

I totally agree. However, and speaking from experience, it is very difficult to 'get in' to schools to do this work, where

Key Facts
- Almost two-thirds of women in prison in the UK are reported to have experienced domestic abuse.
- Around one in four homicides in England and Wales are committed by a current or former partner or relative.

domestic abuse and violence is still seen as a taboo subject for some establishments and parents of children are not always keen for their children to learn about it! But there is no doubt about it...

Knowledge is power!

When Sally was in prison, she attended the Freedom Programme, which is a 12-week group programme for women who have experienced domestic abuse and violence. Sally has said that the programme completely opened her eyes because it made her realise that what she had experienced *was* domestic abuse. Some of you may know that I am a qualified facilitator of the Freedom Programme and have worked with hundreds of women, facilitating this programme. I have witnessed and heard many women say that for the first time, they had realised, they were not to blame for the abuse they had experienced. It is a totally life-changing programme and one which I would recommend to every woman that has experienced domestic abuse. It gives women back some of the control that has been taken from them. It empowers them.

With these new reforms allowing coercive control and physical abuse to be seen as mitigating factors, the criminal justice system now has the ability to take a persons experiences of abuse and trauma into consideration when they are handing down a prison sentence.

Sadly, the new reforms have come too late for hundreds of women who have served or are already serving life sentences for murdering their abusers.

Around one in four homicides in England and Wales are committed by a current or former partner or relative. Of course, murder is a very serious offence and the perpetrators of murder, quite rightly, should receive prison sentences. What would the world look like if no one that commits murder went to prison?! But hopefully, these new reforms will make sure that people who kill as a result of experiencing domestic abuse, and the trauma that comes with it, will at least be seen and treated in a fairer way.

25 July 2023

The above information is reprinted with kind permission from Sharon Bryan Consultancy.
© 2024 Sharon Bryan Consultancy Community Interest Company

www.sharonbryanconsultancy.com

Further Reading/ Useful Websites

Useful Websites

www.durham.ac.uk

www.formentotalk.co.uk

www.independent.co.uk

www.killedwomen.org

www.mariafoggfamilylaw.co.uk

www.metro.co.uk

www.ons.gov.uk

www.refuge.org.uk

www.righttoequality.org

www.sharonbryanconsultancy.com

www.southallblacksisters.org.uk

www.swlondoner.co.uk

www.telegraph.co.uk

www.theconversation.com

www.theguardian.com

www.womensaid.org.uk

Where can I find help?

Below are some telephone numbers, email addresses and websites of agencies or charities that can offer support or advice if you, or someone you know, needs it.

Galop
Galop supports LGBT+ people who have experienced domestic abuse, sexual violence, and other forms of abuse.
0800 999 5428
www.galop.org.uk

ManKind Initiative
01823 334244
www.mankind.org.uk

Men's Advice Line
0808 8010327
info@mensadviceline.org.uk
www.mensadviceline.org.uk

Refuge
0808 2000 247
www.nationaldahelpline.org.uk
www.refuge.org.uk

Respect
Respect provides services for people who are abusive or violent towards their partners or ex-partners.
0845 122 8609
www.respect.uk.net

Sistah Space
020 7846 8350
support@sistahspace.org
www.sistahspace.org

Southall Black Sisters
0208 571 9595
www.southallblacksisters.org.uk

The Freedom Programme
01942 262 270
www.freedomprogramme.co.uk

Women's Aid
helpline@womensaid.org.uk
www.womensaid.org.uk
Scotland: 0800 027 1234; www.womensaid.scot
Wales: 0808 8010 800; Text service: 078600 77333; www.welshwomensaid.org.uk

Glossary

Baiting
A method of provocation. To intentionally make someone angry by doing or saying things to annoy them.

Banter
An exchange of teasing remarks.

Body image
Body image is the subjective sense we have of our appearance and the experience of our physical embodiment. It is an individual's perception of what they look like or what they should look like. It can be influenced by personal memory along with external sources such as the media and comments made by other people.

Bullying
A form of aggressive behaviour used to intimidate someone. It can be inflicted both physically and mentally (psychologically).

Coercive control
The term coercive control refers to the aspects of domestic violence that encompass more than just physical abuse, e.g. psychological behaviour that removes a victim's freedom.

Consent
The act of giving permission for something to happen. This can include medical consent, such as giving permission for a medical procedure to be carried out, or sexual consent - to give permission to a partner to take part in a sexual act.

Dependent children
Usually defined as persons aged under 16, or 16 to 18 and in full-time education, who are part of a family unit and living in the household.

Domestic abuse
Any incident of physical, sexual, emotional, or financial abuse that takes place within an intimate partner relationship. Domestic abuse can be perpetrated by a spouse, partner or other family member and occurs regardless of gender, sex, race, class or religion.

Domestic Abuse Bill
The Domestic Abuse Bill was first announced in 2019. An enhanced draft of the bill was introduced in Parliament in March 2020. The bill aims to improve the effectiveness of the justice system in providing protection for victims of domestic abuse and bringing perpetrators to justice and also to strengthen the support for victims of abuse by statutory agencies.

Elder abuse
Physical, emotional or sexual harm inflicted upon an elderly adult. Elder abuse also includes their financial exploitation or neglect of their welfare by people who are directly responsible for their care.

Family
A domestic group related by blood, marriage or other familial ties living together in a household. A `traditional` or nuclear family usually refers to one in which a married heterosexual couple raise their biological children together; however, changing family structures has resulted in so-called `non-traditional` family groups including step-families, families with adopted or foster children, single-parent families and children being raised by same-sex parents.

Financial abuse
Financial, or economic, abuse involves controlling the victim's finances. This limits the victim's independence and ability to access help, and restricts their ability to leave the abusive relationship. Financial abuse can include withholding money or credit cards, exploiting mutual assets and forcing someone to quit their job or work against their will.

Gaslighting
Psychologically manipulating someone by making them believe their behaviour is at fault.

Harassment
Usually persistent (but not always), a behaviour that is intended to cause distress and offence. It can occur on the school playground, in the workplace and even at home.

Misogyny
Misogyny is hatred of, contempt for, or prejudice against women.

Non-verbal abuse
Can be thought of as a kind of 'psychological warfare' because instead of using spoken words or direct physical violent behaviour, this form of abuse involves the use of mimicry (teasing someone by mimicking them), offensive gestures or body language.

Physical abuse
Physical abuse involves the use of violence or force against a victim and can include hitting, slapping, kicking, pushing, strangling or other forms of violence. Physical assault is a crime and the police have the power to protect victims, but in a domestic violence situation it can sometimes take a long time for the violence to come to light. Some victims are too afraid to go to the police, believe they can reform the abuser (who they may still love), or have normalised their abusive situation and do not realise they can get help.

Refuge
A shelter or safe house, offering a safe place for victims of domestic violence and their children to stay. Refuges can provide practical advice as well as emotional support for victims of domestic abuse until they can find somewhere more permanent to stay.

Sexual abuse
Sexual abuse occurs when a victim is forced into a sexual act against their will, through violence or intimidation. This can include rape. Sexual abuse is always a crime, no matter what the relationship is between the victim and perpetrator.

Sexual violence
Any sexual act that may be considered as degrading, physically aggressive or coercive.

Index

A
abusers 34–35

B
bereaved families 14–17
black women 32–33

C
Challen, Sally 18, 40–41
changing abusers' behaviour 23, 34–35
children 6, 13, 24–25
Clare's Law (Domestic Violence Disclosure Scheme) 38–39
coercive control 2, 7, 18–19, 21, 24
cost of living crisis 10, 35
cycle of violence 13

D
Disclosure Scheme (DVDS) 38–39
Domestic Abuse Act 2021 6, 8, 35

E
education 16, 27, 41
emotional abuse 1, 2, 20–21, 22
excessive (gratuitous) violence 14, 17, 18, 19

F
failure to protect victims 13–17
financial abuse 3, 21
financial support 31

G
gaslighting 21, 22, 23

H
harmful effects 5
harmful practices 3
helplines 10–11, 34–35
homicide *see* murder

I
identifying abuse 1, 2–3, 16, 20–21, 37

L
leaving an abusive relationship 11, 24–25, 26–27, 28–30, 37
love 25
love-bombing 22

M
male victims 8–9, 10–11, 12–13
medical help 29
Men's Advice Line 10–11
murder
    of abusive partner 19, 40–41
    domestic 7, 18, 36
    preventable 14–17
    sentencing 18, 36

N
North America 12–13

P
pandemic 10, 35
physical abuse 1, 2–3, 20
prevalence 5, 6–7, 8–9, 12–13
prison, women in 41

R
refuges 29–30
Respect 34–35
responsibility 4

S
safety when leaving a relationship 28–30
Sally's Law 40–41
same-sex relationships 12
sentencing 18–19, 26, 36, 41
sexual abuse 3, 21, 29
stigma 10–11, 25
support 1, 9, 27, 29–30, 31
survivors of abuse 32–33

T
technological abuse 3, 21
Turner, Tina 32–33
types of abuse 2–3, 6–7, 20–21

V
verbal abuse 1

W
Wade, Clare 18–19, 41
women victims 14–17
Women's Aid 28–30